Weymouth Ferries

The Rise and Fall of a Port

Brian Searle

Published by: Ferry Publications, PO Box 33, Ramsey, Isle of Man IM99 4LP
Tel: +44 (0) 1624 898445   Fax: +44 (0) 1624 898449
E-mail: FerryPubs@manx.net   Website: www.ferrypubs.co.uk

The *Falaise* was built for the Southampton services but after her conversion to a car ferry in 1964 she was placed on the Newhaven-Dieppe route, before she spent her twilight years on the Channel Islands' operations. *(Ferry Publications Library)*

Introduction

This book covers the life and times of the passenger ships and car ferries that have operated from Weymouth for the last fifty years, before conventional ferry traffic from the Dorset port virtually came to a halt.

Brian Jackson produced a fine book about the Great Western Railway steamers at Weymouth some years ago but that story ended effectively with the retirement of the *St. Helier and St. Julien* in September 1960. It is the next fifty years, following the arrival of the *Caesarea* in November 1960, that I have put on record in this title.

Ships have always been popular with the watching as well as the travelling public and I have shared that interest. In fact, for much of my working life, I regarded myself as a privileged person because not only did I reside in Dorset but I actually earned my living on Weymouth Quay watching the boats go by. Had I been asked at the time, I would have said, with much feeling, that it was more than a job, it was a way of life, and part of my existence that I simply would not have wished to change.

I first encountered railway boats shortly after the end of World War II, when my parents took me on several trips on board one of Plymouth's Great Western Railway tenders, either the *Sir Richard Grenville* or *Sir John Hawkins,* both having been returned to peacetime duties. We went on day trips to such exotic places as Looe or Fowey in Cornwall, with a close view of the Eddystone Lighthouse on the way, or just simply a run along the South Devon coast.

When I actually started living in Weymouth during October 1960, I was able to observe at close quarters the two former Great Western Railway steamers, *St. Julien* and *St. Helier* as they awaited their fate. Both vessels had been withdrawn after many years of faithful service. The *St. Julien* was tied up alongside the quay in Weymouth and the *St. Helier* lay at

The **St. Julien** berthed at Weymouth harbour in the early fifties. *(John Hendy collection)*

anchor in Portland Harbour. The Channel Islands' service was being maintained at that time by the *St. Patrick,* known affectionately by everyone connected with railway shipping as 'The Paddy'. She was the last passenger steamer to be ordered by the Great Western Railway and was the third vessel to bear the name. Her maiden voyage from Weymouth to the Channel Islands took place on 4th February 1948 and she remained under Western Region control until transfer to the Southern Region of the British Transport Commission in December 1959.

The *St. Julien* and the *St. Helier* ruled the waves between Weymouth and the Channel Islands for more than a third of a century. They were both completed in 1925 for the Great Western Railway Company and were requisitioned by the Admiralty in 1939 for wartime duties. They came through the hostilities in triumph, despite being in the thick of the action on many occasions, and when the *St. Helier* re-opened the post-war passenger service from Weymouth to the Channel Islands in June 1946, a further period of ten years was to elapse before consideration was given by the British Transport Commission to replace the pair with brand new cross-Channel ferries.

It must be remembered that the *St. Julien* and the *St. Helier,* with summer support from the pre-war *St.*

Patrick (sunk by enemy action in 1941) in their early days, and by the post-war *St. Patrick* in later years, covered the Weymouth-Channel Islands route between them over a very long period. They operated in direct competition with the Southern Railway, whose link with the Channel Islands from Southampton was provided by the three 'Isles', the mail steamers *Isle of Guernsey, Isle of Jersey* and the *Isle of Sark,* all of them classic passenger ferries to the very end of their service.

The story in this book covers the 50 year period from 1960 to 2009, concerning the numerous passenger ships and car ferries which operated from Weymouth up until October 2009. The early part of that era could be termed, with some justification, the post-war heyday of the Dorset port, when the professionalism, enthusiasm and pride of the ships' crews and shore-based staff alike was there for all to see.

I believe that from that moment in November 1977, when Sealink introduced its new service from Portsmouth to the Channel Islands, it was the first nail in the coffin for the port. It was almost inevitable that Weymouth would play 'second fiddle' to Portsmouth, and by the autumn of 1986, Sealink British Ferries had closed its route between the Dorset port and the Channel Islands. Three years later, the Weymouth-Cherbourg link suffered a similar fate, and Sealink abandoned Weymouth. Now only Condor Ferries use this former Great Western Railway port. The size of the Victorian harbour was to speed up its demise and the aggressive marketing and speed of the airlines also did nothing for the port's long-term future. Brittany Ferries' expansion at Portsmouth, Poole and Plymouth with their modern and stylish ships was to dramatically change the scene on the Western Channel as of the early seventies.

Finally I am grateful to Miles Cowsill and John Hendy for their assistance and guidance with this book, and especially for their wide knowledge of the ferry industry in the Western Channel.

Brian Searle
Weymouth
March 2010

The **Ailsa Princess** on passage between Weymouth and St. Helier riding out a gale just off the coast of Jersey. *(Ambrose Greenway)*

1. Setting the Scene at Weymouth

The harbour was a truly fascinating place when I started work in the sixties, with yachts and fishing vessels alongside the various quays, some local yachts afloat at their moorings and two or three paddle steamers gracing the attractive harbour with their presence. The *St. Julien,* was tied up at her berth, having been withdrawn from service during the previous month, together with her 'sister' the *St. Helier,* which I saw later at anchor in Portland Harbour.

I was involved with the arrival of the *St. Patrick* from the Channel Islands, pending the arrival of the two brand new ferries from the Isle of Wight yard of J. Samuel White; the *Caesarea* and *Sarnia.* The former commenced service on 2nd December 1960, with the *Sarnia* arriving in Weymouth to take up station during June 1961, halfway through what was considered to be Weymouth's busiest year for trade.

At the time of my arrival in the Dorset port in October 1960, former Great Western Railway steam engines were still working the tramway and as I had obtained 'digs' in Market Street, I was able to park most conveniently in Governor's Lane car park, for the princely sum of £2 per annum. How times have changed!

The British Railways' operations at Weymouth were headed by the Manager, Bill Salmon, and his assistant, Ronnie Long, but the day-to-day business on the quay was conducted by the Chief Docks Foreman, Ted Le Huray. Born in Guernsey, Ted had joined the Great Western Railway in St. Peter Port as a port docker. During the war he served in Plymouth's Millbay Docks, returning to Guernsey in 1949. He then moved to Weymouth as Dock Foreman

Weymouth Quay in its late Victorian heyday with much activity as horse drawn carriages and an elderly steam train compete for attention with the Great Western's Reindeer. *(John Hendy collection)*

The **St. Julien** dressed overall coming astern at Weymouth. *(John Hendy collection)*

in 1953, and was promoted to the top grade of Chief Dock Foreman in 1960.

Ted Le Huray ruled over the harbour scene at Weymouth for, and on behalf of, the British Rail management, from 1960 to 1974, and his stentorian voice over the loudspeaker system on the railway platform at the quay, when advising passengers about the seating arrangements on the boat trains, will never be forgotten.

He was followed by Bob Stevens, and the late lamented Jimmy Gale, who once advised a Time and Motion Study man surveying working practices on the quay, that the surest way of saving the company money would be for him to resign!

Ron Westhead proved to be the last senior foreman on Weymouth Quay. He was well supported by his supervisors, including the late Len Smith, Leo Plomley, Bill Knibbs and Wally Slade, some splendid members of the Railway Operating Deptartment staff, and a friendly bunch of dockers well looked after by their 'spiritual leader', Dave Cutts. Ron remained in charge on the quay until the collapse of the Channel

Islands' services in the mid-eighties.

As I settled in at Weymouth in the Customs and Excise Office, I began to realise that to be stationed on the quay was more than a job. It was a way of life to be enjoyed as far as possible, whilst always bearing in mind my responsibilities, and those of the people who were employed in different capacities in the harbour. Whilst primarily a book about the passenger ships and car ferries engaged in trade at Weymouth between 1960 and 2009, the story also concerns the personnel on shore, as well as those who manned the ferries, for it was they who helped to make it possible for the ships to trade between Weymouth and the Channel Islands and Cherbourg. Everyone played their part in the shipping scene and everyone had an important slot to fill to ensure the smooth running of the services, particularly those of Sealink, because British Railways and their predecessors had been based in Weymouth for many years, and continued right up until that fateful day in March 1990, when the *Earl Godwin,* as the *Moby Baby,* sailed for the very last time, bringing the curtain down on railway activities at the Dorset port.

Always of interest during the mail boat era was, of course, the use of the mooring boat to assist in turning and/or tying up the cross-Channel ferries. That sturdy boat was employed for many years, right up to the start of Sealink's car ferry activities, but she ended her days by being inadvertently sunk by the *Caledonian Princess*, as the car ferry approached her berth in Weymouth Harbour one day in October 1974. Trapped between the ferry and the quayside, the mooring boat became a total wreck, with her crew being rushed to hospital for checks, fortunately without having incurred any serious injuries.

In 1960, the two senior masters on British Railways' payroll at Weymouth were Captain Jimmy Goodchild and Captain Victor Newton. The former retired in January 1962 when Captain Gerry Cartwright became Senior Master of the delectable *Sarnia,* with Captain Newton remaining as Master of the *Caesarea* until February 1968.

I was privileged to know several Sealink Masters over the years, and one was Captain Paul Baker, now, sadly, no longer with us. Paul had been Master of a number of British Railways' ferries operating from Weymouth and Portsmouth, his last command being the *Earl Granville*.

The first purser I met, as I recall, was Tommy Batchelor, a marvellous fellow whose brother Fred was, at that time, Catering Superintendent for Union Castle Line in Southampton. Sadly Tommy's health failed, and he passed away at a relatively early age without reaching a well-deserved retirement. His daughter later married Ted Renton, a member of British Railways' on-board catering team, to keep up the family interest in the Weymouth ferries.

Mr. Alf 'Pep' Pepper helped shape the future of Weymouth docks when he was Shipping Manager at the port, having been appointed in 1962. Shortly after his retirement in 1973, he was presented with the National Dock Labour Board's certificate for meritorious service, in that he had made a significant contribution to industrial relations in Southampton and Weymouth.

In the autumn of 1974, British Railways' staff waved goodbye to one of the characters on the Channel Isles' route, when Captain Bernard Picot

The **St. Patrick** (II) dressed overall at Weymouth. *(Brian Searle collection)*

The **Isle of Sark** inward bound from the Channel Islands off the Needles. *(John Hendy collection)*

retired after 27 years' service. A chequered wartime career in the Royal Navy was followed by an equally intrepid tour of duty for the railways. He served on every cross-Channel ferry that operated out of Southampton in the post-war years and commanded a number of Weymouth-based ferries, namely the *St. Patrick, Caesarea, Sarnia, Falaise, Normannia* and the *Maid of Kent.* His two principal jobs at Weymouth were inaugurating the roll on - roll off service to Jersey as Master of the *Falaise* in June 1973 and opening the Cherbourg link in command of the *Maid of Kent* in April 1974, when almost at the end of his

The boat train passes down the harbour road in between cars and holidaymakers at Weymouth in the early sixties. *(Late John Lucking)*

long career. Captain Picot was given a rousing send off by his friends and colleagues at a reception on board his last ship, the incomparable *Maid of Kent,* when Mr. George Higgins, who had succeeded Mr. Pepper as Weymouth's Shipping Manager, made the presentation.

Although Sealink (UK) Ltd. did not become a wholly owned subsidiary of the British Railways Board until 1st January 1979, the brand name Sealink had been adopted as early as 1st January 1970, and had become popular with the travelling public. Well-known entertainers, such as Arthur Haines, Joan Turner, Sacha Distel (the famous French vocalist), Jimmy Savile and Alan Randall, were seen passing through the port of Weymouth, with Jimmy Savile being quite a regular traveller during the 1970s, enjoying a friendly chat with local staff on each occasion.

With the introduction of the car ferries in the summer of 1973, when the friendly *Falaise* inaugurated the ro-ro service from Weymouth to St. Helier, our enthusiasm for the new venture was tempered somewhat by the realisation that those incomparable 'sisters', the *Caesarea* and *Sarnia,* faced an uncertain future on the Channel Islands' route. The following year, the *Maid of Kent,* joined the Weymouth 'family', and she quietly and most effectively went about her business, linking the Dorset port with the French port of Cherbourg, albeit on a summer seasonal basis. Sadly, within three years the celebrated *Caesarea* and *Sarnia* had gone!

As the final season for the salubrious *Sarnia* drew to a close in September 1977, British Railways opened the Portsmouth-Channel Islands route in the November and there was a wholesale defection of popular crew members from the Weymouth scene, many of whom were resident in the Channel Islands, and found it much more convenient to serve on the Portsmouth-based ferry. Peter Barton, Billy Wheaton, Tom Barker, Joe Vasse, Don Hills and Tommy Rendell, for example, were all Sealink pursers who had served on the Weymouth circuit for years whilst living either in Jersey or Guernsey and for obvious reasons, they found that they were unable to resist the lure of the new Portsmouth link.

A four-legged celebrity appeared at Weymouth one fine day in the summer of 1978, when the legendary Grand National winner, Red Rum, arrived in a specially designed horse box on board the *Caledonian Princess,* on 1st June. Needless to say, word got around, and he was greeted by a crowd of people, behaving, as always, in an exemplary fashion towards his admirers.

Weymouth's Senior Purser, Eric Symes, one of the smartest officers ever to serve in British Railways' ferries, also retired in 1978, after completing about 50 years at sea. He had joined Union Castle in Southampton at the age of 15 and entered service with the Southern Railway on the old cross-Channel ferry *Hantonia* in 1945. He also performed an important duty as a temporary steward on the car ferry *Autocarrier*, when she was involved in the liberation of Alderney at the end of World War II. Eric was Purser of the *Earl Godwin* shortly before his retirement.

Almost unbelievably, it was impossible in those days for the travelling public to obtain a fresh cup of

The **Maid of Kent** comes astern at Cherbourg from Weymouth during her last year in service. *(Miles Cowsill)*

The **Earl Harold** (ex **Ailsa Princess**) leaves the berth at St. Peter Port for Weymouth in her last year of service on the Channel Islands' operations. *(Miles Cowsill)*

tea on the quay prior to the opening of the Ferry Terminal in 1980. There wasn't even a refreshment kiosk available, but fortunately a delightful lady named Mrs. Janet Stainer brought her tea trolley into action during the busy summer seasons, to provide a little sustenance for travellers as they waited to board the ferry, or the boat train when homeward bound. Janet's refreshment trolley more than supplemented the vending machine on the railway platform and with a pleasing smile, she was able to keep passengers reasonably happy, with a supply of snacks and hot drinks.

With the completion of the Ferry Terminal, a cafe was included with the facilities provided for passengers and local staff alike, and the proprietor was always on hand with a friendly greeting, just like Janet Stainer.

If one was seeking fresh salad, however, one needed to look no further than 2nd Steward Brian Crawshaw on board one of the ferries. He took great pride in supplying Guernsey tomatoes and other fresh vegetables to shore-based staff at Weymouth, and his cabin often resembled a floating greenhouse.

In the late summer of 1980, Sealink's Senior Chief Engineer, Bill Pryde, took his final leave after 31 years' service. Born at Stornaway on the Isle of Lewis, Bill was a quiet unassuming Scot who was an accomplished Scottish country dancer and a keen member of the local Caledonian Society. He was Chief Engineer of the *Sarnia* for many years, but his last cross-Channel ferry was, appropriately enough, the *Caledonian Princess*, and it was on board that ship that a retirement presentation was made to Bill and his wife, by David Vogt, Weymouth's Shipping Manager.

In 1982, vessels belonging to Sealink (UK) Ltd. became involved in the Falklands War, and in support of their colleagues actually operating in the war zone, Sealink employees were given the opportunity to contribute to the South Atlantic Fund, the company itself donation £2,500. In the event, an incredible sum of £3,652 was collected by Cyril Perran, Purser from passengers and crew sailing on the *Earl Godwin, Earl William, Earl Granville* and *Ailsa Princess*, with important contributions from shore-based staff at Weymouth, Portsmouth and Southampton.

Weymouth was in the news again in 1982, when the port was awarded the Lord Robens Shield for the best safety record at work. David Vogt, Sealink's Shipping Manager at Weymouth, received the shield on behalf of his safety committee and staff, from Mr. John Prescott, the shadow spokesman on transport, in the presence of Mr. Len Merryweather, the Managing Director of Sealink (UK) Ltd.

Female staff played a significant part in the day-to-day running of passenger ferries over the years, and one of Sealink's most celebrated stewardesses was Miss Mabel Nicholas. She joined the Great Western Railway's fleet at Fishguard in 1933, and later served in the hospital ship *St. David* in the early days of the war. Later, when the *St. David* sailed for the hostile waters of the Mediterranean Sea, female staff apart from nurses, were encouraged to leave her, and, sadly, the ship came to a violent end in January 1944, being sunk off the Anzio beaches. Ron Long, who was to become Weymouth's Assistant Shipping Manager after the war, was actually a survivor from the doomed *St. David.* Meanwhile Mabel Nicholas had become a passenger guard on the Great Western Railway line between Fishguard and Haverfordwest. She returned to post-war maritime duty on the *St. Patrick*, combining a winter roster at Fishguard, with summer duty between Weymouth and the Channel Islands, and when that ferry was permanently transferred to the Weymouth payroll in 1959, Mabel settled in Dorset. She was awarded the Queen's Coronation Medal in 1953, and finally retired in 1967.

Sealink British Ferries soldiered on with the Cherbourg service and a reduced work force for another three years, but by the end of the decade most of the loyal members of staff had departed, including Shipping Manager, David Vogt, his deputy, Mike Morgan and his assistant, Mike Edwards, all of whom decided to opt for new careers in late 1986. Superintendent Engineer John Carley assumed the mantle of Sealink British Ferries' Port Manager, at a most unfortunate time for Weymouth.

Between 1987, and complete closure of the conventional ferry services in 1990, three companies, British Channel Island Ferries, Weymouth Maritime Services and Westward Ferries, all failed to establish going concerns from the Dorset port. Condor Ferries today remain as the sole operator for passengers and vehicles to the Channel Islands.

Condor Ferries' **Havelet** at the linkspan at Weymouth during her brief period at the port between 2002 and 2003 prior to the delivery of the **Commodore Clipper**. (Barry Watts)

2. Shipping Operations at Weymouth

There is no doubt that the port of Weymouth was a most interesting place in which to be employed during the period under review in this book. Changes in railway shipping practice seemed to take place regularly, the face of Commercial Pier was altered dramatically during those years and to cap it all there was a splendid variety of passenger steamers and car ferries to be seen on the Weymouth-Channel Islands and, later (1974), on the Weymouth-Cherbourg route. Any enthusiast inclined towards cargo vessels, or small craft, would have found much of interest too.

At great risk of repetition, it has to be emphasised that the late 1950s had been a crucial period for the Channel Islands' shipping services generally, and important decisions had to be taken. As early as 1950, air travel to the Channel Isles began to attract passengers to the faster mode of transport. The numbers of visitors to the islands increased considerably after World War II, both by sea and by air, but the sad fact was that as far as the Southern Region of the British Transport Commission was concerned, by 1955 less people were travelling on the ferries than they were by aircraft, and something had to be done to redress the balance.

In its wisdom, the British Transport Commission indicated that it proposed to close the passenger service between Southampton and the Channel Islands, and to concentrate all its efforts at one port, namely Weymouth. Consequently, the three Southampton-based ferries, *Isle of Jersey, Isle of Guernsey* and *Isle of Sark,* would be gradually withdrawn without replacement, and the two veteran former Great Western Railway ships at

A wonderful view of the **Sarnia** on the stocks prior to her launch on 6th September 1960. *(Ferry Publications Library)*

The **Caesarea** during her first season on the Channel Islands' operations. *(Brian Searle collection)*

Weymouth, *St. Julien* and *St. Helier,* would also be retired gracefully, but would be replaced by two new one-class mail steamers.

Following these proposals, there was a flurry of activity. In 1957, an order was placed with J. Samuel White, of Cowes on the Isle of Wight, for two new passenger steamers at a total cost of £3 million, the first to be delivered during the early winter of 1960/61. The following year (1958), the British Transport Commission held discussions with Weymouth Corporation officials regarding the very necessary extensions and alterations to the mail boat berth in the harbour, with the requirement for improved handling facilities, new administration offices for railway staff, new passenger clearing halls for H.M.Customs, and the construction of a third rail track on the pier.

When the British Transport Commission's Shipping Manager in Southampton retired in January 1959, Weymouth's Shipping Manager, Mr. Bill Salmon, took over responsibility for all railway shipping activities at both ports, for it has to be remembered

that the Southampton cargo working to the Channel Islands was to be maintained after closure of the passenger services.

On 26th September 1959, the Channel Isles Boat Express ran for the last time from Weymouth to Paddington, and from 3rd November, the boat trains came firmly under the control of the Southern Region of the BTC with departures from Waterloo to Weymouth operating along the former Southern Railway route via Southampton.

In addition, the summer support steamer, *St. Patrick,* that was technically owned by the Fishguard & Rosslare Railways and Harbour Company, and had remained under Western Region management since nationalisation of the railways in January 1948, was transferred to the Southern Region of the BTC in December 1959, with arrangements to base her permanently at Weymouth.

With the construction of the two new steamers keeping to schedule, the British Transport Commission made its final announcement in the summer of 1960 to the effect that from May 1961, the

Channel Islands' passenger fleet would operate solely from Weymouth and would consist of the two ships being built at Cowes, plus a revitalised *St. Patrick.* Naturally there was sadness and anger in Southampton over the loss of an important passenger route which had been worked by three ferries for many years but in economical terms there could be no dispute.

The old Weymouth faithfuls, the *St. Julien* and *St. Helier,* were withdrawn from service in September 1960, leaving the *St. Patrick* to cover the late autumn working from Weymouth, whilst in Southampton, the *Isle of Jersey* and *Isle of Sark* were sold out of service, leaving the *Isle of Guernsey* to operate a reduced timetable to the islands right up to closure of the route in May 1961.

The *Isle of Guernsey* made her final crossing from Southampton on 12th May 1961, returning to Weymouth on the opening day of the new service on 13th May. The former Southern Railway veteran steamer remained on the Weymouth payroll for four weeks, her final voyage direct from Jersey to the Dorset port coinciding with the arrival of the brand new mail boat *Sarnia,* on 10th June 1961, whereupon the *Isle of Guernsey* destored, and sailed to a lay-up berth in Southampton to await disposal. She was

finally broken up in Ghent in November 1961.

Although some difficulties were encountered during the first summer season in 1961, particularly at peak weekends, when vast numbers of travellers poured through the port of Weymouth and often four boat trains would be marshalled ready to whisk them away to their destinations at Waterloo, Birmingham or Cardiff, it was obvious that the introduction of the new ships had brought success from the very beginning. There were 11% more passengers being carried by the three ferries at Weymouth, than by the six ferries engaged in the Channel Islands' trade from both Weymouth and Southampton during the corresponding period the previous year.

ENTER THE *CAESAREA* AND *SARNIA*

By the end of their first season, the *Caesarea* and *Sarnia,* admirably supported by the third ship, the *St. Patrick,* that had been used mainly on excursions and extra sailings at weekends, had conveyed 200,955 happy voyagers between them, against a total of 181,385 passengers carried on the six ferries in 1960.

The revised weekly timetable for the Weymouth-Channel Islands service commenced on 13th May 1961, with the revamped *St. Patrick* actually covering for the *Sarnia* pending her arrival from the builder's

The **St. Patrick** leaves the berth at St. Helier for Weymouth. The vessel was to spend her 'twilight years' on the Folkestone-Boulogne service. *(Ambrose Greenway)*

Weymouth harbour full to the brim. From left to right: the **Sarnia**, **Caesarea**, **Earl Godwin**, **Maid of Kent** and **Caledonian Princess**. *(Bill Macey)*

yard in Cowes, with the veteran steamer, *Isle of Guernsey,* running the excursion programme and the additional duties at weekends. The new timetables, which operated on Sundays as well during the peak summer months of July and August, produced the best post-war timings between London and Jersey, viz

TIMETABLE WATERLOO TO JERSEY AND RETURN W.E.F. 13TH MAY 1961.

Waterloo depart 08.10 Jersey depart 09.00
Weymouth arrive 11.40 Guernsey " 11.15
" depart 12.30 Weymouth arrive 15.15
Guernsey arrive 16.30 " depart 16.00
Jersey " 18.45 Waterloo arrive 19.35

It is interesting to record that the Waterloo-Weymouth boat train service which commenced on 13th May 1961, was heralded by the re-introduction of the 'Channel Islands Boat Express' roof boards, similar to those used on the Paddington-Weymouth,

with the wording Waterloo-Weymouth added.

Following the arrival of the *Sarnia* in June 1961, the *St. Patrick* was relegated to excursion work and extra weekend duties but her presence on the Weymouth-Channel Isles link was only to last for another two years, because in October 1963 she was transferred to Southampton, leaving the *Caesarea* and the *Sarnia* as the only British Railways' passenger ferries operating on the Weymouth-Channel Isles route.

Until 1967, the redundant French Railways' cargo vessel *Brest,* (assisted by the *Rennes* in 1965), was used during the busy summer months to transport motor cars to the Channel Islands from Weymouth, with the vehicles' owners travelling in comfort on board the mail boats.

Other freight vessels were on charter to British Railways during the same period, including two ships owned by J. Fisher & Son Ltd., and that company's *Lune Fisher* was unusually employed on 23rd May 1964, when she conveyed 12 passengers (the maximum number for an uncertificated ship) to Guernsey, after the scheduled mail boat had

The *Falaise* at full speed off Guernsey inward bound to St. Peter Port. (*Ambrose Greenway*)

departed from Weymouth filled to capacity, leaving those poor unfortunates behind on the quay.

The freight department at Weymouth was extremely busy too. Vast quantities of tomatoes were being imported in a variety of cargo boats, some on charter to British Railways, and it was also the first year in which a new palletisation system was put into operation. The familiar old wooden chip seed boxes vanished and were replaced by new style tomato trays that slotted into pallets, which were easily moved by mechanical handlers, and thus saved a good deal in labour costs. Dock staff also handled large consignments of Jersey potatoes in 1961 and for the first time in many years, cargoes of French broccoli were imported through the Dorset port from St. Malo.

Timber ships could be seen discharging at the Custom House Quay from time to time, and on rare occasions a vessel carrying wine in bulk could be observed pumping ashore its precious liquid cargo into a motorised wine tanker. Not to be forgotten, either, was the diminutive freighter *Audal* which was small enough to berth in the harbour in Alderney,

and used to carry exhaust systems and parts from that island to Weymouth for clearance and onward transit to the Ford Motor Company at Dagenham, usually by rail.

Another important trader in the port in Weymouth in those far off days was John Deheer Ltd. Importers of fertilisers, the company spent some £10,000 to reconstruct its premises on Custom House Quay in order to store 2,500 tons of bulk fertiliser at any one time, and was very much looking forward to an

The car deck of the *Falaise* after her conversion in 1964. (*Kevin Le Scelleur*)

increase in future imports.

The British Transport Commission was dissolved in January 1963, and the British Railways Board came into existence but Weymouth remained largely unaffected by that political change and the *Caesarea* and *Sarnia* continued their successful partnership, creating the cosy feeling that it really was the post-war heyday for passenger shipping at Weymouth, although the threat from the air was never very far away.

The *St. Patrick's* regular support activities at Weymouth ended in October 1963, by which time she had also worked the final season of the British Rail operated inter-Channel Islands and French ports service, which had been inaugurated by the old Southern Railway ferry, the *Brittany*, as far back as 1933, and terminated on 30th September 1963. The *St. Patrick* was later involved in the closure of the Southampton-St. Malo route, before being transferred to the Dover Straits in December 1964. She made a final brief appearance back in Weymouth in August 1968, as a replacement for the *Caesarea,* after the latter had struck an obstruction when entering Weymouth

Harbour, and required attention in a dry dock.

In 1964, the contract for Guernsey's tomato export trade came up for renewal, and British Railways decided to raise their transportation charges quite dramatically. As a result, half of the tonnage was lost to the Commodore Shipping Company, which ran a freight service into Shoreham.

The former Great Western Railway cargo vessels, the *Sambur* and *Roebuck*, were phased out in the mid 1960s after almost 40 years of service, the *Sambur* being the first to go when she was withdrawn in March 1964, laid up in Southampton, and finally towed away for scrapping in a Dutch port on 10th June 1964.

In November 1964, the *Roebuck* found fame when she was chartered by a film company for three weeks, renamed *Galtersund*, and dressed up as a Norwegian coaster for the film 'Heroes of Telemark'. Returning briefly to railway service, the *Roebuck* completed her final crossing from the Channel Islands to Weymouth on 27th February 1965 and was laid up locally before being sold to Lacmots of Queenborough, departing Weymouth for the last time

An unusual visitor at Weymouth, Sealink's dredger **Landguard**. *(Dave Habgood)*

The **Caledonian Princess** makes an impressive view as she cuts through the water inward bound to St. Peter Port. *(Ambrose Greenway)*

on 29th July 1965. She was replaced by the *Winchester* from Southampton on 1st March 1965.

Also that year there was the unusual appearance in Weymouth of the French ferry, *Lisieux,* made redundant on the Dieppe-Newhaven route, and chartered by the French Line (CGT) to launch a summer service between St. Malo and Jersey, the ship's itinerary being extended to include a weekly call at Weymouth.

SEALINK ON THE HORIZON

Major changes to the liveries of British Railway ferries were made in 1965. Gone were the distinctive buff funnels with black topping and black hulls, being replaced by a red funnel with a white double arrow logo, blue hull and grey superstructure. In actual fact, the grey superstructure was found to be hazardous in poor visibility and those ships that had been painted out in that colour, were repainted in white quite quickly. The *St. Patrick* was the first cross-Channel ship to receive the new livery and lost her distinctive G.W.R. stem plate at the same time.

The Channel Islands' passenger figures were finely balanced between sea travel and air travel during the

mid 1960s, but the electrification of the Waterloo to Bournemouth railway line in 1967, encouraged an increase in the numbers travelling to the Channel Islands by sea from Weymouth.

The seamen's strike during the early summer of 1966 badly affected services with passengers having to make alternative arrangements to get to their destinations. In order to boost winter traffic in 1966/67, British Railways introduced cheap weekend 'specials' during the autumn following the lifting of the industrial action.

In 1967, a Channel Islands based company, Jersey Lines, commenced a service between the Channel Islands, Weymouth, Torquay and Cherbourg, employing the old passenger steamer *Brighton,* which had been replaced by car ferries at Newhaven. Renamed *La Duchesse de Bretagne*, she had a major refit before entering service with Jersey Lines. The work included the installation of ramps attached to the sides of the vessel, to enable about 25 cars to be driven on board and stored on the deck, making her the forerunner of the car ferries from Weymouth, no less! The conveyance of motor cars led to a dispute with British Railways, with Jersey Lines finally agreeing to carry only foot passengers from Weymouth, and the company did not return to the Dorset port after the summer season, which ended in September 1967.

On 1st January 1968, the British Rail Shipping and International Services Division (SISD) was established, and in November of that year it was announced that the organisation was to adopt the brand name SEALINK from 1st January 1970. (In fact, the Division was reconstituted on 1st January 1979 as a wholly owned subsidiary of the British Railways Board, and incorporated as Sealink (UK) Ltd.)

The French cargo boat *Brest* finished her charter work on the Weymouth-Channel Isles route in the autumn of 1967 and in the ensuing years, British Railways' own freighters, the *Elk* and *Moose,* were given the job of transporting passengers' cars to the islands from Weymouth, whilst the vehicles' owners travelled in comfort on board the *Caesarea* or *Sarnia.* That type of traffic was to cease in 1972, and virtually at the same time, all sea freight working was transferred to Portsmouth.

Direct travel between the United Kingdom and the Channel Islands was not governed by the law concerning that dreaded disease, rabies, but sometime during the late 1960s, British Railways introduced a new company regulation concerning the carriage of dogs to and from the Channel Islands, and this stated that dogs accompanying passengers would only be accepted on the mail boats if confined in one of the kennels provided on 'B' deck.

Shortly after that ruling was introduced, a very small elderly lady came on board the *Caesarea* at Weymouth, clutching the tiniest dog one could ever wish to see. She was immediately tackled by the purser of the day, who politely reminded her of the regulation of which she was apparently unaware. The purser, however, was adamant that the rule could not be ignored, and the little old lady was accompanied to 'B' deck by a steward. When shown the kennels she immediately selected one, and squeezed into it with her dog, obviously preferring the company of her pooch to her fellow travellers!

Townsend Thoresen's *Free Enterprise II* was chartered to Sealink in 1980. She is seen here arriving at the Dorset port from the Channel Islands. *(Miles Cowsill)*

Onlookers watch the **Caledonian Princess** as she clears the harbour entrance from St. Peter Port for Weymouth. *(John Hendy)*

CAR FERRY SERVICES TO THE CHANNEL ISLANDS

Following lengthy discussions between the British Railways Board and the local authorities in the Dorset port and in St. Helier, Jersey, it was decided to open a new ro-ro working between the two ports. With ramps being constructed in each harbour during the winter of 1972/73, the service was inaugurated on 1st June 1973 with the *Falaise* under the command of Bernard Picot. The States of Guernsey weren't interested in the enterprise initially, but they became involved later, and the ro-ro service from Weymouth to Jersey was extended to St. Peter Port in June 1974. This virtually coincided with the opening of a completely new route from Weymouth to Cherbourg in April 1974, employing the *Maid of Kent*.

In March 1974, there was a shake up in managerial circles, and the H.Q. of Sealink's Channel Islands' services was moved from Liverpool Street, London to South Western House in Southampton, which was ideally situated, with easy access to Weymouth, Portsmouth and the Channel Islands.

The summer of 1974 saw the introduction of the 'Night Flyer' excursion programme from Weymouth to St. Helier, involving overnight travel in both directions, and allowing a full 15 hours in Jersey. It

began with a 00.30 departure from Weymouth, arriving in St. Helier at 06.00, departing from there at 21.45 and arriving back in Weymouth at 05.00 the next day. The fare of £8 included 200 cigarettes and one litre bottle of spirits duty free, and there were optional extras such as a supper for 95p and a coach tour of the island.

These 'Night Flyers' were extended to Guernsey in 1975 but the price of the excursion had been increased slightly to £10. Passengers obtained the same benefits as those on the Jersey trips, but unfortunately, the time ashore in St. Peter Port was limited to the ship's timetable. Nevertheless, the Guernsey excursion proved to be quite popular with the travelling public.

TOWNSEND THORESEN

It was at this time that Townsend Thoresen, operating on routes from Dover and Southampton, looked at the possibility of using Weymouth in order to expand their services to France, and letters were exchanged between Weymouth Corporation and that company in the summer of 1974, which gave rise to a strong rumour that there might be a challenge to Sealink's monopoly at the Dorset port in the summer of 1975.

In fact, Captain Holden, Weymouth's Harbour Master, wrote to Townsend Thoresen on 23rd August 1974, "I confirm the availability of the linkspan and ferry terminal for the period from approximately the last week in June 1975 to the first week in September 1975, from 17.30 to 18.30 daily, for a ship not exceeding 113 metres in length, 20 metres in beam and 4.3 metres in draught."

This letter, which was acknowledged by Townsend Thoresen, seemed to be quite innocuous in itself and did not appear to give the independent company any particular right to a berth in Weymouth Harbour, but it was probably the catalyst which encouraged Townsend Thoresen to pursue the matter through the courts, after Weymouth Council, at a meeting on 31st October 1974, decided against allowing the company access to the linkspan or the ferry terminal.

Townsend Thoresen warned that they would instruct their solicitors to sue the Weymouth Borough Council in the High Court for the loss of anticipated earnings on the proposed service, indicating that they believed that the Council had agreed in principle in the August 1974 letter, to the effect that they, Townsend Thoresen, would be entitled to ro-ro facilities at Weymouth during the summer of 1975 and that the Council had withdrawn the 'offer' as a result of pressure from British Railways, when the latter apparently told the local council in no uncertain terms "you can have us or Townsend Thoresen, but not both". The independent company estimated that their losses, as a result of the Weymouth Council's decision taken in October 1974, were likely to be in the region of £259,000.

The hearing opened in January 1977, and the Q.C. for the Council denied that his clients had ever entered into a contract of any kind with Townsend Thoresen. Mr. Justice Donaldson, carefully listened to all the evidence, and ruled against Weymouth Council, holding that worthy body to be in breach of contract but leaving the two sides time to agree on a figure of compensation for the plaintiffs, and ordering the Council to meet 75% of the costs.

Twelve months later, on 19th January 1978, a total of £259,000 damages, plus interest and costs, were awarded against Weymouth Council. Members of that local government organisation met in February 1978,

The **Caesarea** slowly manoeuvres onto her berth at Weymouth. Note the small boat to the bow of the vessel taking the landing ropes. The car ferry **Normannia** can be seen at the linkspan loading for her sailing to Guernsey. *(Joe Ward)*

A busy scene at Weymouth harbour with the **Maid of Kent**, **Caesarea** and **Svea Drott**. *(Ambrose Greenway)*

and in a secret session, reached a decision to enter into negotiations with Townsend Thoresen and following discussions with that aggrieved company, an agreed figure of £255,000 was to be paid in three instalments, the municipal body thus saving £4,000 plus £20,000 in costs and £76,000 in interest, not an insignificant sum.

This brought to an end a very embarrassing period in Weymouth Council's relationship with British Railways at a time when the nationalised concern was quietly preparing a coffin for the Dorset port in faraway Portsmouth, a south coast port in which the enthusiastic and ambitious ferry company, Townsend Thoresen, was already becoming quite a force.

FIVE SHIPS FOR WEYMOUTH

For the time being, however, it was Sealink all the way at Weymouth, and in October 1974, and again in February 1976, there was the impressive and never to be forgotten sight of five Sealink passenger/car ferries berthed in Weymouth Harbour at the same time.

By 1976, the Weymouth-Cherbourg service had been successfully running for two years and during

the late autumn of that year, Sealink introduced package trips to France, calling them the 'French Connection'. For £26, passengers could obtain a return ticket for a voyage on the *Maid of Kent* from Weymouth to Cherbourg, sample evening dinner in a French restaurant before a comfortable night's rest in the Hotel du Louvre, in a room with full facilities, then enjoy a continental breakfast with a short period of relaxation in the French port, before the afternoon return sailing to Weymouth. Included in the price of the package was a litre bottle of whisky and 200 cigarettes, obtainable on the journey home.

British Railways' own dredger, the *Landguard*, undertook its largest ever contract for an outside organisation when it was chartered by the local council at Weymouth in 1977, to dredge the harbour to the depth required for the operation of the railways' Channel Islands and Cherbourg services. Based at Harwich, the *Landguard*, under the command of Captain Sid Davies, left the Essex port at the end of February, and within 24 hours she was commencing the job of removing about 35,000 cubic metres of spoil from the harbour at Weymouth, for dumping at sea. The whole operation took six weeks and was a complete success.

In November 1977, British Railways decided to open a 'second front' to the Channel Islands. Rumours had started in Weymouth in June 1976, about a possible new passenger link from Portsmouth but Mr. John Chapman, Weymouth's Shipping Services Manager denied that any plans had been formulated for such a service although he did admit that B.R. were constantly reviewing the situation in the light of developments, and their long-term plans included the safeguarding of business by countering any competition. In the event, the splitting of the Channel Islands' trade failed and was operationally catastrophic as far as Weymouth was concerned, leading eventually to the demise of Sealink's involvement at the Dorset port.

All was not lost, however, and Sealink's Assistant Manager at Weymouth, Mr. John Warley, managed to persuade the Ford Motor Company, which had a backlog of Fiesta cars, manufactured in Spain and lying on the continent, to use the facilities of an under employed Weymouth. This proved to be an excellent piece of entrepreneurial work by John Warley, and by mid-February, car carriers full of trade cars were arriving in the Dorset port for discharge. In fact, by August 1979, the port of Weymouth had handled 15,400 trade cars landed from a total of 28 specialist car carrying vessels, plus 1,100 cars shipped on board the *Maid of Kent* at Cherbourg at various times during that period. Ford were delighted with the facilities provided at Weymouth and with the teamwork displayed by Sealink staff, the agents Abbey Hill of Yeovil and the local Customs authorities ensured speedy clearance of the vehicles. For example, a ship carrying 700 trade cars could be berthed, discharged and back at sea again in less than 12 hours.

For a time, FIAT cars became regular imports, being transported by train from Turin to Cherbourg, and then shipped on board the *Maid of Kent* for landing at Weymouth, usually in quantities of about 50 at each sailing. Those numbers were driven on board the ship in Cherbourg as and when convenient,

The **Caledonian Princess** swings in the harbour at St. Peter Port following her arrival from Jersey. (*John Hendy*)

and dock personnel in the French port must take some credit too, because the difficulties experienced in loading trade cars during a quick turnaround of the ferry, were overcome by the efficiency and enthusiasm of the local staff who had never previously had to deal with that type of traffic in such a short space of time.

As mentioned earlier, the Shipping & International Services Division (SISD) disappeared at the end of 1978, the division being reconstituted as a wholly owned subsidiary of the British Railways Board, and incorporated as Sealink (UK) Ltd. on 1st January 1979, and it wasn't long before a very interesting summer excursion programme embracing Weymouth, Cherbourg and Southampton was arranged, following an agreement between Sealink (UK) Ltd. and the Cunard Line. The vessels involved were the Cunard flagship, *Queen Elizabeth 2* and the *Maid of Kent* for Sealink initially, although she was replaced by the *Ailsa Princess* in 1982. Passengers could select their direction of travel, and the options are fully

described in the relevant chapter on the two Sealink car ferries.

Following financial losses, and increased fuel costs in 1979, Sealink's management decided to alleviate the problem a little, certainly in the Western Channel, by slowing down the ferries to and from the Channel Islands by one knot. As a result, the booked arrival times into Weymouth were changed from 06.00 to 06.15 for the night ferry, and from 15.00 to 15.15 for the afternoon arrival. In addition, motorists travelling on the *Earl Godwin* and the *Caledonian Princess* were asked to pay a fuel surcharge of £4.

John Warley brought a smile back to the gloomy face of Weymouth when, following his splendid performance in obtaining contracts for the importation of trade cars into the port during its lean time early in 1978, he made the news again when he dreamed up a method of conveying passengers' baggage from a pick-up point on Commercial Pier, to the linkspan, for loading on to the car deck of the service vessel.

A wonderful view of Weymouth in the early seventies with the **Sarnia** and **Maid of Kent** loading for their sailings to Jersey and Cherbourg. *(Ferry Publications Library)*

The *Maid of Kent* pictured at Cherbourg on her last sailing to Weymouth in September 1981. *(Ferry Publications Library)*

There were obvious problems for foot passengers arriving at Weymouth to board the car ferry for the Channel Islands or Cherbourg as it was extremely difficult to carry heavy suitcases up the gangway at that time. With that situation in mind, it was Sealink's Assistant Shipping Manager who proposed that those passengers arriving for embarkation, should leave their heavy baggage at the end of the platform on Commercial Pier, usually under the supervision of Garnett Mahoney, who was always superbly attired in white coat and cap, and sporting a fresh carnation in his buttonhole. The baggage was then loaded on to a set of loosely coupled wagons, known throughout the Sealink world as 'Warley's Wonders', and driven around to the ramp for shipment on the departing ferry.

BONUS FOR WEYMOUTH

On a lovely day in the autumn of 1979, we witnessed the engaging experience of Sealink's publicity seeking 'train versus road' race from Waterloo to Weymouth. The diesel locomotive hauling the boat train was named 'Isle of Jersey' for the day, to celebrate the fact that over 100,000 'Bonus Breakaway' holidays had been sold, a 50% increase over the previous year. The naming ceremony was performed by Miss Jersey, with international racing driver, Alain de Cadenet, resplendent in a Sealink pullover, in close attendance.

The train departed from Waterloo at precisely the same time as seven luxury cars and seven motorcycles, the drivers of the road vehicles being honour bound to observe all speed restrictions along the way. Astonishingly, the train and vehicles (except one Rolls Royce, which was unavoidably delayed) arrived at Weymouth railway station almost simultaneously and journalists who had sampled both modes of transport, went on to join the outward bound ferry for a 'Bonus Breakaway' in Jersey.

On 14th July 1980, the Minister of Transport, Norman Fowler, announced proposals to introduce private capital into the main non-railway subsidiaries

An impressive view of the *Earl Granville* off Jersey inward bound to St. Helier. *(Kevin Le Scelleur)*

of British Railways, and Sealink (UK) Ltd. was to be the first of those subsidiaries to be privatised, the subject being described fairly fully elsewhere in this book.

Still looking at the trials and tribulations of the year 1980, it is interesting to relate that Truckline used Weymouth for a few nights in September. The French company was based in Poole and their ferry, *Coutances,* had an unfortunate accident in her home port on Friday 19th September which caused considerable damage to the linkspan and put it out of action. Sealink's Shipping Services Manager at Weymouth, David Vogt, came to the aid of the Poole company by offering use of the local ramp for a short period of time during unsocial hours and Weymouth's staff contributed tremendously to the success of the venture, by clearing the ro-ro ferry company's arrivals and departures during the early hours of each morning throughout the emergency.

With 14 cases of foot and mouth disease confirmed in nearby France early in 1981, it was almost inevitable that it would carry to the Channel Islands on thermal currents and in March 1981 Jersey

was declared an infected area with a small number of cases. There was grave concern in the neighbouring island of Guernsey, where stringent measures were put in place to try and prevent an outbreak there. Those measures included disinfectant pads being placed at the bottom of gangways of ferries arriving in St. Peter Port, with similar pads positioned at the yacht marina and at the airport. Control of fishing vessels was increased, and all vehicles arriving in St. Peter Port by ferry, had their wheels sprayed thoroughly with disinfectant. Similar steps were taken in Weymouth and Portsmouth.

FAREWELL TO THE MAID OF KENT

In the autumn of 1981, the *Maid of Kent,* was withdrawn from service and later dispatched to a breaker's yard. Strapped for cash, the company decided not to entertain plans for a new vessel to replace the 'Maid' on the Weymouth-Cherbourg route but looked at existing tonnage, and after some deliberation, chose the *Ailsa Princess* from the Irish Sea. One thing she did have in her favour, of course,

The **Earl Harold** contends with the rough seas off the Channel Islands outward bound for Weymouth. *(Ambrose Greenway)*

was her ability to carry high-sided vehicles, so the prospect of ro-ro freight on the Cherbourg link certainly looked promising.

What looked decidedly gloomy in the autumn of 1981 was the fact that Sealink intended to slash car ferry sailings from Weymouth to the Channel Islands in 1982, with a drop of 51 departures on the previous year's programme. Sailings were maintained during the peak season, but in the winter and spring periods, the figures were reduced considerably. It was all very unsatisfactory, because at a meeting between Sealink (UK) Ltd. and the Weymouth & Portland Borough Council's Harbour and Industry Committee in July 1981, Derek Shorter, Sealink's Channel Islands' Shipping Manager, had said that rumours circulating about a future decrease in services at Weymouth were not correct, so the later news in September was received with incredulity. The Harbour and Industry Committee Chairman, Eric Webb, described the news as disappointing, a bit of an understatement really, because we all knew at the time that Weymouth was playing 'second fiddle' to

Portsmouth, and any cuts in services would be applied to the Dorset port in the first instance.

The summer seasonal sailings to Cherbourg were opened in April 1982 by the *Ailsa Princess*, and by June she was well into the routine of linking Weymouth daily with the French port, when the French Railways (SNCF) suddenly announced that they had decided to withdraw from the partnership with Sealink (UK) Ltd., leaving full control of the route, including all aspects of marketing, to pass to the British organisation.

The *Ailsa Princess* continued to give a good account of herself during the summer of 1982, the one blip being the fire on the car deck as vehicles were about to disembark in Cherbourg on 24th July.

Non-landing day out cruises from Weymouth to Cherbourg were again introduced on a daily basis from 24th May to 1st October 1982, an added attraction being the free litre bottle of wine which was included in the £9.75 fare.

Unfortunately, the Falklands War broke out in April 1982 and the popular Sealink (UK) Ltd./Cunard

In 1987 Sealink chartered the **Svea Drott** and later purchased the vessel and renamed her to the **Earl Godwin**. The Scandinavian ship is seen here at the berth at Weymouth during her first few weeks in service. *(Colin Caddy)*

Line combined cruises to Cherbourg, first conceived in 1979, employing the *Maid of Kent* from Weymouth, and the *Queen Elizabeth 2* from Southampton, were abandoned, due to the Cunarder's call up for use as a troop ship in the South Atlantic campaign. Following the cessation of hostilities in mid-June, the 'Q.E.2' was returned to her owners and a short programme of cruises to and from Cherbourg was arranged with Sealink in August and September 1982.

An interesting railway and sea anniversary occurred on 24th May 1982. It was the 125th anniversary of the rail and sea link between London and the Channel Islands via Weymouth, which had opened in 1857 following completion of the railway line to the Dorset port. Celebrations were marred, however, by a one-day strike by Waterloo train drivers, which resulted in the cancellation of the Weymouth-Channel Isles boat train.

Unfortunately, because of the strike, Sealink called off the planned reception at the Ferry Terminal, but children from a local school all appeared in fancy dress for what should have been an historic occasion and they did manage to get in a tour of the *Earl Godwin* before the car ferry's afternoon departure to the Channel Islands.

Also as a way of celebrating the special rail and sea anniversary, Sealink re-introduced the 'Jersey Night Flyer', in which it was possible to enjoy up to 15 hours of sunshine by departing from Weymouth on the night ferry at 23.45, and returning from the Channel Islands on the scheduled ferry into Weymouth on the following night, during the period 11th June to 24th September 1982. The fare of £19.50 included a litre bottle of spirits and two litre bottles of table wine, and proved to be quite attractive, with children travelling at reduced rates as they were not permitted to have spirits and wine. For interested passengers, it was also possible to book an island coach tour for £3.95 extra.

On the 8th March 1983, history was made by British Railways at Weymouth, when 105 new Metro and Mini cars were brought from the British Leyland factory in Birmingham to Weymouth Quay on a 21 wagon train, for shipment to the Channel Islands on board the *Earl Godwin*. The train was confronted by thick fog on arrival in the port at 06.00 but after a slow start the fog cleared and allowed the *Earl Godwin* to proceed along the Dorset coast on a four hour publicity trip for travel agents and other interested parties, to promote the summer's services to the Channel Islands and Cherbourg.

The *Earl Godwin* returned to Weymouth Harbour during the afternoon, and later loaded 50 of the export cars delivered by the train earlier in the day, for discharge in the Channel Islands. The remaining vehicles were exported on the following night's sailing. This venture was repeated on one further occasion, but the train did not terminate at Weymouth Quay, and the cars were offloaded near the Junction, being subsequently transferred to the quay by road, and shipped on board the export vessel.

JERSEY NIGHT FLYERS

Also in 1983, Sealink introduced 'The Extended Service' during the peak holiday months of July and August. This special working, which commenced on 2nd July, was provided at the busy weekends, and it involved Weymouth's *Earl William* and the Portsmouth-based *Earl Granville* making calls at Cherbourg in addition to their regular Channel Islands visits, thus giving travellers to Cherbourg the bonus of a third arrival in, and departure from, Weymouth at the height of the summer season.

The *Earl Granville* would leave Portsmouth at 23.00 on the Friday evening, arriving first in Jersey and then on to Guernsey, on the Saturday morning. She left St. Peter Port for Weymouth at 10.25, arriving in the Dorset port at 14.30 on the Saturday, and following a quick turnaround, the ferry departed to Cherbourg at 15.30, returning to Weymouth after a speedy discharge and loading in the French port, at 00.30 on the Sunday. Leaving Weymouth for St. Helier late on Sunday morning, the *Earl Granville* returned from there directly to Portsmouth, to complete 'The Extended Service' cycle.

Weymouth's *Earl William* performed a similar role in the reverse direction, but it has to be said that during those busy weekends, the ferries found it difficult to keep to their somewhat punishing timetables, though from a strictly financial viewpoint, the service got off to a fine start, with 12,700 passengers and 2,500 cars being carried during the first full weekend in July 1983.

An independent freight company, Weybourg, was set up in the summer of 1983, and opened for business between Weymouth and Cherbourg on 2nd October. Sadly, Weybourg Shipping Company was unable to secure enough trade to make the venture a viable one, and it closed down in December 1983, after less than three months in operation.

In contrast, Sealink (UK) Ltd. actually had a bumper season in 1983, particularly with the 'Bonus Breakaway Holiday', which broke all records with over 60,000 bookings in the first eight months of the year. Another success story was the 'Night Flyer' excursion programme, which recorded over 58,000 bookings during the same period. Not surprisingly, between 13th January and 30th March 1984, Sealink introduced non-landing cruises on Friday night sailings from Weymouth, in an attempt to boost passenger figures during the normally slack winter period. Those cruises were known as 'Casino Fun Cruises', and in addition to being able to watch well-known local entertainers performing en passage, travellers over 18 years of age received a gaming voucher worth £5 included in the fare of £14.60. The ferry was scheduled to return to Weymouth on Saturday afternoon.

At about the same time, intending passengers could pick up a 'Weekend Bonus Breakaway', which included two nights either in Jersey or Guernsey, plus a litre bottle of spirits and two litres of table wine, for the inclusive fare of £58. Alternatively, travellers could obtain one night's dinner, with bed and breakfast in St. Peter Port, for the bargain price of £24.50, by departing from Weymouth on the 13.30 sailing on Tuesdays or Thursdays, on what was known as the 'Guernsey Sampler Break'.

PRIVATISATION

With privatisation looming, Sealink embarked on a major livery change for the fleet; the first ferry to show off the new image being the *St. Nicholas,* and she was presented to the public at Dover on 27th March 1984. Gone was the old British Railways' double arrow sign on the funnel, and in its place was a gold logo made up from the letters SL, and looking similar to a naval officer's braiding.

The Weymouth-based ferries were not repainted during that first season but were dealt with as they became available for annual refit or temporary lay up, in the course of the ensuing winter period. Each vessel was given a white hull, with a bottom line band of blue, and with a gold logo on its funnel. The change was to give the impression of cleanliness, attractiveness, quality and reliability in an attempt to ensure that Sealink was first choice in the ferry world.

Privatisation of Sealink (UK) Ltd. was completed in July 1984. Just before that momentous occasion, however, something happened which was to have far reaching effects on Sealink trade between Weymouth, Portsmouth, the Channel Islands and Cherbourg.

Early in May 1984, top-level talks had been held in Jersey and Guernsey between the local authorities and Brittany Ferries, regarding the possibility of opening a new service between the Channel Islands and Portsmouth. A spokesman for Brittany Ferries verified that talks had indeed taken place on 2nd May 1984 but that no decision had been reached. In St. Helier, the harbour authority confirmed that there was spare ramp time available should another operator come forward with a request to use it. It looked quite ominous for the newly privatised company.

James Sherwood, the President of the newly formed company, Sealink British Ferries, intimated in his New Year Message to staff on 11th January 1985, that £5 million was to be spent on upgrading the ferries at Portsmouth and Weymouth, for the proposed 'Starliner' service (from Portsmouth) and the 'Sunliner' service (from Weymouth), both due to commence in May 1985.

The 'Starliner' service was, as the name implied, a night working to the Channel Islands. The vessels employed on that link, the *Earl Granville* and the *Earl William*, were refurbished in Denmark at a cost of £5 million and when they returned to the fray, instead of the normal accommodation for 1,200 passengers, there were first class cabins for only 400 passengers, who were to be provided with candle lit dinners and super breakfasts but at a very much increased cost. A

Originally built as the **Viking II** for Thoresen Car Ferries, Sealink acquired the vessel in 1982 and renamed her the **Earl William** for their Channel Islands' operations. *(Ambrose Greenway)*

family of four paid £337 for a mid-week return voyage.

The 'Sunliner' service from Weymouth provided day sailings, and was aimed at the cheaper end of the market. With a return fare of £99 for a family of four, it had a moderately successful trading summer, with the financial return almost evenly balanced at the end of the season. Not so at Portsmouth where a deficit of £6.5 million was incurred during the first year. Sherwood and his marketing team completely misread the requirements of the travelling public, particularly at Portsmouth, where demand for more costly, first class style of shipboard accommodation never materialised. Pressure also built up from a real competitor, Channel Island Ferries, who opened a ro-ro service from Portsmouth on 29th March 1985 at much lower travel cost.

Channel Island Ferries, the new challengers on the route, with the *Corbiere*, who were backed up by Brittany Ferries, offered a cabin for four persons for £104 in the high season, with suitable reductions at other times of the year. There simply was no contest!

Still with his New Year Message of 11th January 1985, Sherwood went on to say that with the likely entry of a rival company on to the Portsmouth-Channel Islands circuit, which happened on 29th March, Sealink British Ferries considered that they were no longer under any obligation to operate loss-making winter services on the Channel Islands' routes because those had only been undertaken in the past in the absence of competition. The future of Weymouth, in particular, began to look very bleak.

In conclusion, Sherwood said that the former Isle of Man Steam Packet Company's vessel, *Manx Viking,* was to be transferred from the Heysham-Isle of Man link to replace the *Ailsa Princess* on Weymouth's seasonal route to Cherbourg. However, the *Manx Viking,* became unavailable in the fleet, and the Swedish car ferry *Thjelvar* was hastily chartered for a few weeks to open the Cherbourg service, before a more permanent charter was agreed with the Belgian Government for their *Prins Philippe.* The Belgian ferry arrived at Weymouth on 6th May 1985, and remained at the port throughout the rest of the summer.

The 'Starliner' and 'Sunliner' services were a failure and simple figures for a comparison between

1983, when the 'Extended Service' was introduced, and 1985, the first year of operating the other two much vaunted services, shows quite a fall in the numbers of passengers carried. Details of the numbers of passengers carried on the routes from Weymouth are shown below:-

PASSENGERS/C.I. ROUTE PASSENGERS/CHERBOURG ROUTE

	C.I. ROUTE	CHERBOURG ROUTE
1983	368,850	138,260
1985	155,780	91,057

Regarding the Channel Isles' programme, Sealink British Ferries said that the drop in numbers was largely caused by the rescheduling of sailing times since privatisation, which made it impossible to run the popular 'Night Flyer' excursions to the islands. Why on earth was a reasonably successful timetable changed, heralding a drastic drop in support for the ferries at Weymouth?

SEALINK S LAST YEAR

A new Chairman of Sealink (UK) Ltd. and Director of British Ferries Ltd. was appointed at the end of 1985, in succession to Len Merryweather, who took a much needed retirement after being at Sealink's helm through difficult times. He was replaced by Charles Lennox-Conyngham, who had spent his entire working life in sea transport and so was not lacking in experience for his new role.

The New Year (1986) opened with a great deal of stormy weather in the English Channel which was a taste of things to come at Weymouth, and not only as far as climatic conditions were concerned. Without the knowledge of the Sealink board, the local management of Sealink British Ferries announced a change of appearance for the company's vessels operating in the Western Channel from both Weymouth and Portsmouth, with the legend 'British Ferries' replacing the existing 'Sealink British Ferries', although in actual fact the changes only lasted for one year. It is believed that the the renaming of the company was never referred to top managment.

The first blow to strike Weymouth happened early in the year, when all the Sealink British Ferries' services were suspended at the port during the week commencing 17th February 1986. The Weymouth-based ferry, *Earl Godwin* was at refit in Glasgow, with the *Earl Harold* (ex *Ailsa Princess*) serving in the Irish Sea at the time, and the relief ferry at the Dorset port, the *Earl William,* was recalled to Portsmouth to replace the *Earl Granville,* that had been sent on a promotional exercise to the Pool of London. Fortunately Weymouth operations returned to something like normal within a week, with the *Earl Harold* arriving in the port to re-open the Channel Islands' link on 24th February, and the *Earl Godwin* returned from her refit in March, to open up the seasonal route to Cherbourg.

The much publicised 'Sunliner' service from Weymouth was now reduced to one ship, the *Earl Harold,* with the *Earl Godwin* maintaining the Cherbourg link. Sealink British Ferries were hard pressed for cash at this time, and one innovation early in the season was to offer free return trips during the whole of June, provided that travellers brought teddy bears with them. The cost for the bears was £10, passengers obtained his or her ticket free, and it was valid for a month. Sealink British Ferries were so keen to promote the 'Teddy Bear Trips', that the Weymouth booking office also offered a 'bear for hire' service, to encourage more passengers to take advantage of the scheme.

Weymouth had a moderately successful summer season in 1986, which included a popular open day on 20th April, when some 2,800 visitors clambered on board the *Earl Godwin* at the quayside but at Portsmouth, the company faced an uphill battle to recover from the disastrous 'Starliner' season the previous year. It never did recover, and the trading season ended in a calamitous way, particularly at Weymouth, where the service to the Channel Islands was suspended on 30th September 1986 with an appalling loss of jobs. That day was indeed 'Black Tuesday' for the Dorset port, when Sealink British Ferries' bosses were accused of displaying the worse face of capitalism and of selling Weymouth out. As the crisis deepened, crew members of the *Earl Godwin* at Weymouth prepared to 'sit in' on the

The ***Earl Godwin*** proved to be an excellent ship for Sealink on their Channel Islands' operations. After the demise of the company to Jersey and Guernsey in 1986, she was later sold to Moby Lines and still remains in service in 2010. *(Ambrose Greenway)*

vessel, until they received assurances from management that either their jobs were secure, or that proper arrangements for redundancy payments would be forthcoming.

Meanwhile, the *Earl Harold* was drifting around in Weymouth Bay whilst waiting for a berth in the harbour and finally left the area to dock at Portsmouth at 20.00 under the command of Captain Craythorne flying the skull and crossbones from the mainmast. The *Earl William* arrived in Guernsey from Portsmouth and her Master decided to remain on the ramp and 'sit things out'. In fact she did not depart St. Peter Port until 18th October and she berthed in Weymouth later that day. Shortly afterwards, the *Earl Harold* arrived coastwise from Portsmouth to lay up with the *Earl Godwin* and *Earl William* for an unspecified period.

The people of Weymouth rallied around with food, gifts and goodwill messages to help the staff carry their protest into November, but following six weeks of talks, the dispute came to an end on 11th November 1986, when an agreement was reached, and those who had lost their jobs with Sealink British Ferries at Weymouth, collected their redundancy cheques. As they left the quay office for the last time, with little prospect of immediate employment, they looked back on a once thriving, but now deserted, terminal, with three ships lying idle. It was heartbreaking!

Following the Zeebrugge disaster in March 1987, the government decided to press ahead with stringent regulations to improve the safety of all British merchant vessels, particularly ro-ro ferries. After examination it was found that four Sealink British Ferries' vessels failed to measure up to the new safety standards, with a lot of detailed work required to bring them up to scratch. The cross-Channel ferries affected were the *Earl Granville* and *Earl Harold*, the others being the *Tynwald* (ex *Antrim Princess*) and the ro-ro freighter *Darnia*. The company was given a deadline in which to correct deficiencies, and it was decided to dispose of the *Tynwald* and the *Darnia* within the period allowed.

On Friday 10th April 1987, Condor commenced activities at Weymouth, with their fast ferry service.

It all began with a farce, however, as Condor staff and Weymouth dockers wrestled with the mooring ropes as the first ferry, *Condor 7*, arrived in the port from the Channel Islands, to begin her programme of daily sailings.

In the absence of genial Sandy Gore, Sealink's long-serving Berthing Master at Weymouth, who had retired with the closure of the conventional car ferry services to the Channel Islands the previous year, we witnessed some amazing scenes on the quay as the Condor manager, David Norman and his staff, all wearing black suits, insisted on helping the local dock staff to moor the ferry. In David Norman's view, Condor personnel were responsible for berthing the *Condor 7*, with assistance, if required, provided by the Weymouth dockers but the local secretary of the T&GWU declared most emphatically, that it was the dockers' job to secure the vessel alongside the quay. Fortunately common sense prevailed, and the matter was eventually settled without bloodshed.

Sealink British Ferries continued with their summer only working from Weymouth until October 1989, before closing its services completely at the Dorset port. The *Earl Godwin* performed the last rites before proceeding to Portsmouth where she also closed the Cherbourg link with the Hampshire port in December 1989. She returned to Weymouth on the day before Christmas Eve to lay up, and she remained alongside the quay until March 1990, when she was sold to Italian interests and renamed *Moby Baby*.

Several other companies attempted to open new services from Weymouth right up to and including 1990, and those efforts are dealt with briefly in chapter five. All failed financially within a short space of time, except British Channel Island Ferries (BCIF), but that company abandoned its regular Portsmouth-Channel Isles route, and the summer only service from Weymouth, which had opened in 1987. Instead it opted for Poole as its UK terminal in January 1989, leaving Condor Ferries to carry on with its hydrofoil service as the sole method of transporting passengers by sea from Weymouth to Jersey and Guernsey.

3. Other Passenger & Freight Services

COMPAGNIE GENERALE TRANSATLANTIQUE (FRENCH LINE) 1965

As a shipping company with a history of running great liners across the oceans, it was a bit surprising to see the mighty French Line trying its luck in the Channel Islands' trade but in July 1965 it did just that when the company chartered the French Railways' (SNCF) ferry *Lisieux*, which had just been made redundant on the Dieppe-Newhaven link, and embarked on a series of excursions from St. Malo to the Channel Islands, Weymouth and Torquay.

The charter period lasted for some 12 weeks, although Weymouth was only involved for seven weeks between 13th August and 1st October 1965. Each Friday during that short period, the *Lisieux* took day trippers from Weymouth to Guernsey, and on return would sail overnight to St. Malo, arriving in the French port on Saturday morning.

Whilst the activities of the *Lisieux* added much interest to the port workings at Weymouth, the French Line venture into the cross-Channel excursion world was not very successful in financial terms, and was not repeated.

JERSEY LINES - 1967

In 1967, Jersey Lines was a small Channel Islands based company operating a former Great Western Railway Plymouth tender, the *Sir Richard Grenville*, renamed *La Duchesse de Normandie,* on a service between St. Helier and Granville.

The company's very enthusiastic Managing Director, N.F. Cowasjee, had, however, purchased the former British Railways' fuel-thirsty ferry *Brighton* (another redundant Newhaven-Dieppe passenger ferry) in December 1966, renamed her *La Duchesse de*

The **Lisieux** was used by Compagnie Generale Transatlantique for their operations from St. Malo to the Channel Islands, Weymouth and Torquay. The ship was built for the Newhaven - Dieppe route and is seen arriving in the French port. *(John Hendy collection)*

The **La Duchesse de Normandie** was built as the **Sir Richard Grenville** for the Great Western Railway. *(John Hendy collection)*

Bretagne and fitted her out for services from Torquay and Weymouth to the Channel Islands and Cherbourg during the summer of 1967. The refit included the provision of side ramps, to facilitate the loading of cars that were carried on the open deck.

The company had bad luck from the very beginning, and when they were refused permission to load vehicles at Weymouth other than those approved by British Railways, car ferry services from the Dorset port had to be cancelled and those arrivals and departures transferred to the Torquay timetable. Passenger only services continued from Weymouth until the end of the season but Jersey Lines did not return to the Dorset port in 1968 and unfortunately went bankrupt the following year.

BRITISH CHANNEL ISLAND FERRIES (BCIF) - 1987 AND 1988

British Channel Island Ferries was first mooted in the autumn of 1986, following the introduction of a ro-ro service between the Channel Islands and Portsmouth in March 1985 and the closure of the Weymouth-Channel Isles link by Sealink British Ferries on 30th September 1986. Following the suspension of Sealink British Ferries' services between Portsmouth and the Channel Islands at the same time, attempts were made by Channel Island Ferries and Sealink British Ferries to reach agreement on the provision of one ship each, on charter to a new company to be established as British Channel Island Ferries (BCIF) using the *Corbiere* and the spare

The **Brighton** seen at Newhaven alongside the quay having recently arrived from Dieppe. *(Late Douglass Hoppins)*

Dover/ Folkestone ferry *Vortigern.*

Unfortunately, Sealink British Ferries failed to harmonise with the NUS and the Officers' union, and as a result were unable to proceed with the offer of a vessel for the new company. Channel Island Ferries then took out an injunction in the High Court, which they won, with an interim agreement with Sealink British Ferries to continue to trade as British Channel Island Ferries, employing the updated *Corbiere,* on a regular timetable between Portsmouth and the Channel Islands.

British Channel Island Ferries also introduced a summer only service to the Channel Islands from Weymouth on 15th April 1987, using the chartered Cypriot car ferry *Baroness M,* repainted and renamed *Portelet* for her new duty. The ship was none other than the former P&O ferry *Lion,* late of the Ardrossan-Belfast and Dover-Boulogne routes and sold to the Mediterranean at the end of her useful career in the Dover Straits. Despite early technical difficulties, when the *Cornouailles* was urgently dispatched from Poole to assist the newly chartered ship, BCIF had a fairly successful season running

from the Dorset port and, indeed, elected to charter the vessel again in 1988.

The *Portelet* was due to open the new season on 6th April 1988 but prior to that the *Corbiere,* on her regular voyage to Portsmouth from the Channel Islands, had been diverted to Weymouth with engine trouble on 30th March. Following the disembarkation of passengers and cars, urgent repairs were carried out at Weymouth before she sailed for the Channel Islands, fully loaded, on 3rd April. Her departure finalised a unique occasion at Weymouth, which saw

A rare view of BCIF's **Corbiere** at Weymouth in April 1987. *(Late Hugh Brooks)*

Possibly the most disastrous period for BCIF was the charter of the **Portelet** on the Jersey and Guernsey services following the demise of Sealink British Ferries' operations the previous year. The Cypriot-registered vessel is seen here at Weymouth pending her afternoon sailing to Guernsey. *(Miles Cowsill)*

two British Channel Island Ferries' passenger/car ferries tied up in the harbour at the same time.

The *Portelet* commenced its second summer routine as scheduled on 6th April and continued operations until 1st October, with BCIF closing its office doors at Weymouth for the last time shortly afterwards. The company was later to terminate its activities at Portsmouth and opened its new link between Poole and the Channel Islands in January 1989.

WEYMOUTH MARITIME SERVICES LTD. — SUMMER 1989

Weymouth Maritime Services Ltd. was a small shipping company formed in the spring of 1989 by a zealous Jerseyman, Captain Ivan Allo. It filled a vacuum in conventional car ferry services between Weymouth and the Channel Islands, which had been there since BCIF closed its Weymouth office in October 1988.

Negotiations with Weymouth & Portland Borough Council and the various authorities in the Channel

Islands were positive, approval was obtained and the new season was scheduled to commence with a 23.30 departure from Weymouth on Friday 3rd May 1989. Weymouth Maritime Services chartered the *Bohus* of Scandi Line in Norway and renamed her the *St. Julien*, a name not unfamiliar with shipping enthusiasts in Weymouth and the Channel Islands. She was a relatively small car ferry of some 1,561 gross tons, small enough, in fact, to berth in the harbour at Alderney, and two calls there were included in the weekly schedule.

Despite the undoubted enthusiasm of Captain Allo and his colleagues, an august body which included Captain Bill Roberts, formerly with Sealink British Ferries as Operations Manager, problems were encountered from the start. In addition, it became increasingly more difficult to generate sufficient interest with the travelling public and/or freight organisations, to make it a successful enterprise.

By 3rd October 1989, the date set for the start of the winter programme, which had already been

The **St. Julien** was chartered by Weymouth Maritime Services Ltd in 1989 for their rival service to that of BCIF. *(Miles Cowsill)*

advertised, the service had been closed down with heavy financial losses, and the vessel was repossessed by her Norwegian owners, finally leaving Weymouth on 28th October 1989. Sadly, Weymouth Maritime Services went into liquidation in March 1990.

WESTWARD FERRIES — SUMMER 1990

Westward Ferries was the name of the operating arm of offshore contractors Lowline Ltd. It was set up at Weymouth in the summer of 1990 to re-open the Cherbourg link (closed in October 1989), using a former Royal Fleet Auxiliary, *Sir Lancelot*, which had been purchased from the Ministry of Defence by the parent company, and renamed the *Lowland Lancer*. With a yellow hull, white upper works and a buff funnel, she was soon nicknamed 'The Yellow Peril' by the Weymouth shipping fraternity, and was arguably the most unusual car ferry to appear in the Dorset port.

She sailed on her inaugural voyage to Cherbourg on 18th July 1990 but soon found that demand for private car and lorry and/or trailer space was poor,

particularly from Cherbourg, where negotiations for an improved timetable failed to provide a satisfactory period at the loading jetty and brought no benefit to Westward Ferries whatsoever. This contributed massively to the financial problems of the company. As a result, the *Lowland Lancer* made her final crossing from Cherbourg to Weymouth on 29th October, when the service was suspended and the vessel laid up.

An unusual visitor to Weymouth was the former Royal Fleet Auxiliary ship **Sir Lancelot**. She was chartered by Westward Ferries and renamed the **Lowland Lancer** for their Cherbourg service in 1990. *(Brian Searle collection)*

CONDOR FERRIES

Following the collapse of Sealink British Ferries' service to the Channel Islands in September 1986, attempts were made made by BCIF to bring some life to the route with a summer only service during 1987 and 1988. Meanwhile in the spring of 1987, Condor Ferries started their operations at Weymouth, with the first arrival on 10th April with their hydrofoil the *Condor 7*. She operated successfully in tandem with the *Condor 9*, until the arrival of the much larger car-carrying vessel the *Condor Express*. The company ceased operating from Weymouth in 1997, with a final voyage from the Channel Islands on 28th February with the *Condor Express*, and after her arrival in Weymouth at 17.00, she landed passengers and cars before sailing 'light' to Poole.

After a disappointing season at Poole in 1997, the company returned to Weymouth in May 1998, employing the newly commissioned *Condor Vitesse*, and from October 1998, Condor moved their UK Terminal for their all round year service to the Channel Isles, back to Weymouth.

Meanwhile, following the takeover of BCIF by Condor, the *Havelet* arrived in Weymouth on 6th March 1994, she was employed offering an overnight, year round service from the Weymouth to the Channel Islands. She had to be withdrawn from service in September 1996 due to certain defects which needed to be rectified under SOLAS regulations. The *Havelet* was laid up in Portland Harbour for a lengthy period, while the *Condor 12* operated the winter service from Weymouth.

The *Havelet* was later brought back into service again as back-up vessel for the fast craft operations during bad weather. She was based in Weymouth for a year between September 1998 and October 1999, until the arrival of the new *Commodore Clipper* for the Portsmouth and the Channel Islands operations.

The *Havelet* was laid up in Weymouth for a time, before being sold. She left Weymouth in August 2000 for Bar in the Adriatic under her new name of the

Following the demise of BCIF, Condor Ferries concentrated their operations at both Weymouth and Poole. This view shows the **Condor 12** outward bound to the Channel Islands with the conventional car ferry **Havelet** preparing to enter the harbour. *(Barry Watts)*

In September 1980 Truckline were forced to use Weymouth as their UK port when the linkspan at Poole was out of action. This view shows the **Coutances** and also the **Caledonian Princess** at the lay-by berth. (Joe Ward)

Sveti Stefan. For the last ten years, the *Condor Express* and *Condor Vitesse* have remained on the Weymouth service.

FREIGHT SERVICES

TRUCKLINE FERRIES — AUTUMN 1980

Truckline Ferries commenced freight operations from Cherbourg to Poole in June 1973. In September 1980, Truckline sought permission to use the ramp at Weymouth for a short period, as one of the company's freighters, the *Coutances,* had caused some £200,000 of damage to the linkspan at Poole, whilst berthing on Friday 19th September. The linkspan was put out of action, and the vessel was also damaged, the latter requiring repairs which were subsequently carried out in Cherbourg. The Sealink (UK) Ltd. Shipping Manager at Weymouth, David Vogt, was asked for urgent assistance to act as agent to facilitate cargo handling during the week commencing Monday 22nd September. With authority given, modifications to the existing ramp at Weymouth were carried out by the local Marine

Workshop staff.

High-sided vehicles, trailers and trade cars were dealt with by Weymouth's dock staff most efficiently between Monday 22nd September and Wednesday 24th September 1980 inclusive, boosting Weymouth Harbour's income considerably in a relatively short period of operations. Truckline's ferry, *Purbeck,* was employed on the service, and because of Sealink's own ferry commitments necessitating use of the ramp during daylight hours, Truckline Ferries were given full use of it at night for loading and discharge.

Sealink even provided accommodation for a small group of Truckline staff, who actually took up 'residence' in Assistant Freight Manager Alan Jones' office temporarily.

WEYBOURG SHIPPING COMPANY — AUTUMN 1983

This company was set up in 1983 to run a freight service between Weymouth and Cherbourg. The company's proposals were approved by Weymouth Corporation at a meeting on 21st April 1983, when the local authority agreed to spend some £25,000 to modify the ramp and provide facilities in the port. The company appointed Sealink's former senior master at Weymouth, Captain Michael Hurd-Wood as their Operations Manager.

At the time, Weybourg proposed to purchase or charter a French vessel named *Leon,* which was inspected in a dock in Marseilles in June 1983, and seemed to be exactly what was required for the job. Repairs to the ship, and negotiations for her charter were rather protracted, however the plan was to employ the *Leon* and to rename her *Weybourg I* but this never came to fruition.

Instead of the *Leon,* the newly appointed shipping company decided to take a Danish ferry, the *Mercandian Explorer II,* on a 90-day charter and to inaugurate their service on Sunday 2nd October 1983. Despite some early friction, the company reached an agreement with the NUS to employ the Danish ferry, pending the arrival of a British registered vessel.

The chartered Danish vessel arrived in Weymouth Bay on 20th September and lay at anchor before entering harbour for ramp trials on 24th September. She made a satisfactory trial run to Cherbourg on 27th September, and sailed on her inaugural voyage for Weybourg with a small amount of freight on 2nd October.

The ship's working timetable was simple. Departure from Weymouth was at 20.00 daily, a relaxed voyage across the Channel allowing her to berth and discharge in Cherbourg at 08.00 the following day. Arrival back in Weymouth was scheduled for 18.00, with two hours on the ramp for discharge and loading, prior to departure again at 20.00.

Weybourg Shipping had also hoped to provide spaces for private cars to be shipped on board the *Mercandian Explorer II* with the owners being conveyed to Hurn Airport and accommodated locally overnight, before flying to Cherbourg to rejoin their vehicles at the French port.

Unfortunately, loadings were poor from the start of operations, and after two unsuccessful months, Weybourg Shipping Company ceased trading, the programme was abandoned, and the chartered freighter *Mercandian Explorer II* left Weymouth for the last time in the early hours of 20th December 1983.

The company announced at the time that it would return to full-time trading after the 1983 Christmas break, but, sadly, that was not to be, and six months later, on 12th June 1984, Weybourg Shipping Company passed into history.

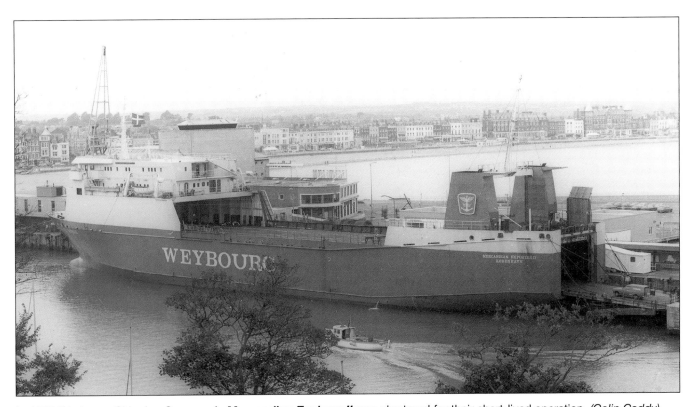

In 1983 Weybourg Shipping Company's ***Mercandian Explorer II*** was chartered for their short-lived operation. *(Colin Caddy)*

4. Ships of Weymouth

CAESAREA & SARNIA

Ordered by the Southern Region of British Railways as early as 1957, the *Caesarea* and *Sarnia* were built by J. Samuel White and Company Ltd. of Cowes on the Isle of Wight, at a cost of £1,500,000 each, and were the last mail boats to be designed and constructed for the Channel Isles' service from Weymouth, replacing those very popular former Great Western Railway veterans, *St. Julien* and *St. Helier,* both ships having been in action continuously on the route, apart from the war years, from 1925 to 1960.

The eventual construction of the new mail ships came after lengthy discussions concerning the future of the Channel Islands' services from both Weymouth and Southampton, with the British Transport Commission deciding to close the passenger route from Southampton, thus rendering the old Southern Railway steamers, *Isle of Jersey, Isle of Guernsey* and *Isle of Sark* redundant. Freight workings from both Southampton and Weymouth were to continue as before, but from 13th May 1961, it was intended that all passenger services to the Channel Islands would run from Weymouth, using newly built ships and working a revised timetable, together with the refurbished and freshly appointed one class steamer, *St. Patrick,* handling the additional weekend sailings and excursion trips during the summer season.

The *Isle of Jersey* was sold out of service and the *Isle of Sark* went to the breaker's yard, but the *Isle of Guernsey* was held in reserve to complete the final winter schedule (1960-1961) from Southampton. As it so happened, the *Sarnia* was not due to enter service until the spring of 1961, so the *Isle of Guernsey* was

The **Caesarea** goes down the slipway at Cowes on 29th January 1960. *(John Attwood collection)*

The *Sarnia* arrives at St. Helier inward bound from Weymouth. The launch in front of the vessel prepares to come alongside to take her ropes. *(Ambrose Greenway)*

dispatched to Weymouth as cover for her from 13th May until her arrival in the port.

Almost identical in design, the sisters were the largest vessels ever built for the Channel Islands' service, and were the largest that could berth in St. Helier Harbour at that time. The overall length of each ship was 322 feet, their beam being 51 feet and the loaded draught 13.5 feet. With a gross tonnage of 4,174 tons, they were also the largest passenger ferries to operate from Weymouth up to the end of the 1960s.

The vessels had raked stems, rounded sterns and a single funnel, the funnel being designed to obviate any nuisance caused by fumes, which was always likely to occur in adverse weather conditions. Both steamers had twin screws, with a balanced rudder aft, and a bow rudder to facilitate easier movement in confined waters, such as when entering or leaving port. The rudders were operated by rotary vane type steering gears of AEG manufacture, the power being supplied by hydraulic pumps driven by electric motors.

The *Caesarea* and *Sarnia* were each powered by two Pametrada steam turbine engines, which gave a total output of 8,500 S.H.P. Two oil fired water-tube boilers, fitted with super-heaters, supplied steam at a working pressure of 350 lbs. per sq. in. to the main turbines and auxiliary machinery. Three 225 kW. 225 volt D/C diesel driven generators supplied electricity for all lighting and power, with 60 miles of electric cable laid throughout each ship. The latest type of navigational aid was also installed, to assist the Master on the bridge to combat fog and other hazards at sea.

With safety very much in mind, the ships were fitted with the latest type of sprinkler systems and were also divided into fireproof zones, each zone containing additional equipment to detect and fight fire. In the event of a major emergency, six glass fibre lifeboats (four hand propelled and two powered by diesel engines) and 45 inflatable life rafts were carried in each vessel and life jackets were provided for each passenger and member of the crew.

The *Caesarea* and *Sarnia* could carry 1,400 passengers, and had a crew of 78. One class accommodation for passengers provided a new

The **Caesarea** at full speed off the coast of Jersey in 1971. *(Ambrose Greenway)*

concept in railway boat travel and was designed with a strong emphasis on comfort, which was essential to meet the ever growing threat of faster transportation by air. There were two continuous decks, main and upper, plus a promenade deck, a boat deck and a navigational bridge deck. Passengers had access to all decks except the latter and all public rooms were arranged either on the main, upper or promenade decks. Three superb lounges attractively panelled out in Lebanon Cedar and Andaman Padauk, provided perfect relaxation for up to 396 travellers.

On each almost identical ferry, the smoke room and bar was situated at the forward end of the promenade deck, and was panelled throughout in Andaman Padauk and East Indian Rosewood. Armchairs and fixed seats provided the necessary comfort for 96 passengers, with tables finished in rosewood to complete the picture of seaborne tranquillity. At the other end of the promenade deck, travellers could relax in the buffet/bar, where there was seating for 117 passengers.

On the upper deck was the popular buffet/lounge. Panelled in cedar, this attractive public room could seat a maximum of 132 people at any given time. The ship's shop was also situated on this deck, and in the shop one could purchase fancy goods, cosmetics and souvenirs of the voyage. The ship's spacious restaurant was also to be found on the upper deck. It was finished in English yew throughout, and catering staff could deal with 110 diners at any one sitting in extremely comfortable and pleasant surroundings. The cafeteria was immediately below it on the main deck and it was here that the self-service buffet provided seating for 142 passengers to supplement the restaurant service. Apart from those extensive facilities for passengers in public rooms, there were also sheltered positions on the open decks, where seating was available for 400 passengers when sailing conditions were reasonable. Hardy travellers could be found there at any state of the weather or time of day.

Sleeping accommodation consisted of two luxury cabins with private facilities, and 25 double and 12 single cabins. They were well appointed and provided a high degree of comfort for the occupants. In addition to those cabins, there were two separate 22-berth sleeping lounges for ladies and gentlemen, and many reclining seats situated in lounges and other areas throughout the ship.

About 20 motor cars could be carried in the holds of the new steamers, after being hoisted on board by crane. Over the years, passengers watched anxiously as their vehicles were loaded on board, but it was an extremely rare occurrence for one to be dropped, either on the quayside or straight into the hold of the ship.

The two passenger steamers, *Caesarea* and *Sarnia,* were maintained to a high standard throughout the 1960s and when important reconstruction work was required on both vessels, the British Railways' Marine Workshops at Weymouth were delighted to receive instructions to undertake the work locally during the winter of 1970/71. The job, under the general supervision of Reg Voller, the Marine Workshops' foreman, was completed after seven weeks' intensive activity on each ship, which was a credit to the local staff at Weymouth.

The stern lounges, and the A deck port and starboard observer sections in each vessel were gutted, and the whole area transformed in time to help boost the new seat reservation system being introduced for the spring of 1971. New lime green poly floor was laid in the new lounges, strip lighting fitted, and two toned brown and grey plastic upholstered chairs fixed to the floors, to provide seating accommodation for 160 people. The A deck port and starboard observation areas were similarly treated. During the following winter period (1971/72), the C deck tea bars on both the *Caesarea* and the *Sarnia* were converted to self-service buffets. This work was carried out to utilise all the existing space to the advantage of the travelling public, by giving them a greater range of drinks and snacks from a larger counter area, thus reducing the waiting time for the hungry voyagers.

Sadly, within three years the great partnership between the *Caesarea* and the *Sarnia* would be broken up, with the *Caesarea* completing her final year on the Channel Isles' working in 1975, before moving to the Dover Straits. The demise of the *Sarnia* on the Weymouth-Channel Islands route was to follow two years later.

CAESAREA

The arrival of the new vessels into service was anticipated with great excitement, and the *Caesarea* was the first to emerge from the builder's yard, being launched on 29th January 1960 by Lady Coutanche, the wife of the Bailiff of Jersey. Following completion and trials, she arrived in Weymouth on 12th November 1960, and four days later, the new steamer was presented to a party of VIPs and members of the press, on a Channel cruise.

The inaugural cruise of the *Caesarea* to the Channel Islands on 18th November commenced at 01.15 on that November day. The brand new *Caesarea*, under the command of Captain Victor Newton, and with Chief Engineering Officer Henry Hodder in charge 'down below', slipped her ropes at Southampton, and set out on her first visit to Jersey and Guernsey.

The *Caesarea* arrived in St. Helier at 09.30, and was met by the Bailiff, Sir Alexander Coutanche, and his reception committee. Lunch was followed by a short afternoon cruise for the invited guests, the official Jersey visitors to the ship and the passengers from the United Kingdom, all of whom left the ship shortly after 19.00, the latter being conveyed to the Grand Hotel, where they remained as guests until the evening of Sunday 20th November. In the afternoon, between 14.00 and 17.00, members of the general public were invited to look around the ship, and what a popular decision that proved to be, with hundreds of Jersey citizens swarming over the new ferry.

The *Caesarea* left St. Helier at 07.30 on Monday 21st November, and arrived in St. Peter Port at approximately 09.30, the local reception committee and invited guests arriving on board, and remaining for lunch at 12.30. The vessel was opened to the public between 16.00 and 18.00, and shortly after that time, access to the ship was closed, and a motor coach arrived to convey the visitors to Government House, for a cocktail party at the invitation of the Lieutenant Governor. They later attended a dinner at the Old Government House Hotel.

On the following day, Tuesday 22nd November, the *Caesarea* was again opened up to members of the public between the hours of 09.30 and noon, and then with all local visitors back on shore, she left St. Peter Port at approximately 12.30, arriving back in Southampton in time for the VIPs to take up their reserved seats on the 19.15 train to Waterloo.

The *Caesarea* later sailed for Weymouth, where she was stored up and made ready for entry into the Channel Islands' trade, sailing on her maiden revenue-earning voyage from the Dorset port with a fairly quiet night departure on 2nd December, which contrasted sharply with the enthusiasm shown on the two introductory cruises.

Six months later, the *Caesarea* was on hand to welcome her new sister, the *Sarnia,* to Guernsey on 14th June 1961, because her arrival in St. Peter Port, on the scheduled run between St. Helier and Weymouth, was less than $2\frac{1}{2}$ hours after the start of the inaugural visit of the *Sarnia* to the island, and the occasion provided a unique opportunity to see the two sisters together.

Apart from the odd teething problem early in her career, the *Caesarea* settled down well to provide (from June 1961) a marvellous partnership with the *Sarnia* on the Weymouth-Channel Isles route,

interrupted only for annual inspections and some minor accidents. The first incident occurred on 29th July 1964, when the *Caesarea* sustained slight damage after hitting a rock at the entrance to St. Peter Port Harbour in Guernsey, but delay to services was minimal.

On 22nd August 1968, however, there was more serious damage to the hull, which was holed after the ferry struck an obstacle whilst entering Weymouth Harbour. The *Caesarea* was dispatched to a dry dock in Southampton for urgent repairs, being relieved by another old Weymouth favourite, the *St. Patrick.* In between these two incidents, the *Caesarea* had been switched to Dover on 14th December 1966, when she replaced the *Invicta* on the prestigious 'Golden Arrow' service for a six-week period.

In 1972, the *Caesarea* required urgent repairs to her propellers, after she became entangled with lobster pots off Guernsey in thick fog on 19th July. She was dry docked in Falmouth for a few days whilst the work was carried out, so the veteran steamer, *Maid of Orleans,* arriving light in Jersey direct from Dover, took over the working during that

The **Caesarea** dressed overall at Weymouth prior to entering service. *(Brian Searle collection)*

This interesting view shows the bridge on board the **Caesarea**. *(John Attwood collection)*

busy period in mid-summer.

Much later, on 9th March 1973, the *Caesarea* grounded whilst entering harbour at St. Helier, damaged her fuel tanks and was withdrawn immediately for inspection, leaving the route temporarily without a ship. A mild state of panic broke out in the ranks of the Sealink managerial staff at Weymouth, but, fortunately, the stern-loading car ferry, *Holyhead Ferry I,* was heading down the English Channel bound for her home port of Holyhead after a spell of detached duty in the Dover Straits. She was conveniently diverted to Weymouth that very day in order to take the night departure from the Dorset port to the Channel Islands. Because of her length, the *Holyhead Ferry I* was unable to berth in St. Helier, and called at St. Peter Port, Guernsey only on that isolated occasion, returning to Weymouth on 12th March 1973 to complete the round voyage.

It wasn't until 1973 that the *Caesarea* made her first visit to Cherbourg, when she carried 600 passengers on an excursion to the French port on Thursday 12th April. The passengers boarded the ship at Weymouth at 23.00 on 11th April, and she arrived in Cherbourg at 05.45 on the following day, allowing a considerable period of time for the excursionist to explore the French port, before departing late in the day for a 05.00 arrival in Weymouth on Friday 13th April.

Less than three months later, on 1st June, a new era dawned for the port of Weymouth, when the old Southern Railway steamer, *Falaise,* which had been converted into a car ferry in 1964, opened a new ro-ro service from the Dorset port to St. Helier in Jersey. The ro-ro link to St. Peter Port in Guernsey followed a year later, and these new services marked the beginning of the end for those incomparable twins, *Caesarea* and *Sarnia*.

Another grand tradition vanished from the scene in the port of Weymouth and the Channel Islands in October 1973, when the *Caesarea* and *Sarnia*, each lost the title 'Royal Mail Ship'. Air transport to the Channel Islands had 'captured' the first class type of mail some years earlier, but the ferries had continued to carry parcels and large quantities of printed material for the GPO. Now, with the ro-ro ferries

The late evening sun catches the **Caesarea** outward bound from Jersey. *(Ambrose Greenway)*

The **Caesarea** inward bound to St. Helier off Noirmont Point. *(Ambrose Greenway)*

arriving on the scene without provision to carry mail in the orthodox manner, it fell to the *Caesarea* to make the final run to the Channel Islands with bags of the Queen's Mail on 5th October 1973, returning with the last conventional shipment from the Islands on 8th October. After this both the *Caesarea* and the *Sarnia* ceased to fly the Royal Mail Pennant.

The *Caesarea* kept going at Weymouth for a further two years, but was withdrawn from the Channel Islands' link in October 1975. Captain Alun Milward was in command for her last voyage, and he had with him as honoured guests, her first master, Captain Victor Newton, who had served in her right up until his retirement in February 1968, and her first chief engineer, Mr. Henry Hodder. The *Caesarea* arrived in St. Peter Port from St. Helier, on a full tide at 10.00 on 6th October 1975.

For her final call, a small reception was held on the bridge of the mail steamer, attended by His Excellency the Lieutenant Governor of Guernsey, Vice Admiral Sir John Martin and Lady Martin, Martin Miller, the BR Manager in Guernsey, and Captain M.H. Mellish, ADC to His Excellency. Then, with a relatively peaceful departure, without music or vast crowds on the quayside, the magnificent *Caesarea* slipped her moorings and left St. Peter Port at 11.00 on her last scheduled voyage to Weymouth, with the words 'farewell' flying from the flags of the Signal Station, and friendly blasts from the sirens of the ships in port.

It had been a glorious period in which the modern car ferry could never hope to compete in terms of comfort and service to its passengers, except, perhaps, the one and only *Maid of Kent,* but, sadly, all good things come to an end, and after wintering over at a berth in Weymouth, the majestic *Caesarea* left the Dorset port for Dover in February 1976, where she replaced the ageing *Maid of Orleans.*

Fortunately for Dorset steamship enthusiasts, the *Caesarea* had not quite finished with the Weymouth-Channel Islands scene. In April 1978, she was recalled from the Dover Straits to run in tandem with the *Normannia* for a three-week period, after the veteran

The Corbiere lighthouse makes an impressive backdrop with the **Caesarea** inward bound to St. Helier. *(Ambrose Greenway)*

car ferry's passenger certificate had been suspended due to the deterioration in the standards of accommodation caused by an embarrassing internal oil leak. Private motor vehicles were conveyed on the *Normannia*, whilst their owners were once again able to relax in comfort on board the peerless *Caesarea*, commanded once again by a Weymouth master mariner, Captain Tom Bill. It was all over on 6th May 1978, however, when the *Caesarea*, and, indeed, the *Normannia*, sailed from the Channel Islands to Weymouth for the very last time, bringing to an end, classic steamer operations on the route.

The *Caesarea* returned to the Straits of Dover, where she operated for two more years, her final voyage in Sealink colours being a charter trip organised by Captain Mike Bodiam on behalf of the Dover Rotary Club, with all proceeds going to the RNLI.

Purchased by Superluck Enterprises Inc. of Panama, whose Managing Director was Hong Kong ship owner, Mr. Willie Wong, and renamed *Aesarea* by dropping the 'C', she left Newhaven on 20th December 1980, for a new life as a floating hotel and conference centre in Hong Kong. Her new crew of Chinese and Filipino nationals had taken over the ship at Newhaven, and, unfortunately on departure, she hit the Railway Quay with considerable force, doing some £2,000 worth of damage. After some delay, the *Aesarea* left the Sussex port for Hong Kong, where she arrived on 10th February 1981, after a long voyage through the Mediterranean Sea, the Suez Canal and the Indian Ocean. The early proposals never came to fruition, however, and she was laid up in Hong Kong, pending a decision as to her future. The *Aesarea* was still out of commission two years later, when typhoon 'Ellen' struck the area on 9th September 1983, and she was driven ashore. She was refloated the following day, but remained laid up as a dead ship for a considerable period of time.

In fact, she was never steamed again, and the end came when she was unceremoniously put to the torch in a South Korean breaker's yard in 1986. It was a tragic and inglorious exit for a magnificent steamer, which had served British Railways and Sealink in the English Channel, with pride and distinction for so many years.

The **Caesarea** pictured at full speed off Portland. *(Ambrose Greenway)*

An outstanding picture of the **Caesarea** off the Jersey coast outward bound for Weymouth. *(Ferry Publications Library)*

The **Caesarea** at the end of her career at Boulogne pending one of her last departures to Folkestone. *(Miles Cowsill)*

SARNIA

The *Sarnia* was launched on the 6th September 1960 by Lady Arnold, the wife of the Bailiff of Guernsey, Sir William Arnold, in a special ceremony at J. Samuel White's yard in Cowes on the Isle of Wight. Completed in May 1961, the elegant *Sarnia* arrived on the Weymouth stage on 10th June, her appearance coinciding with the final voyage of the *Isle of Guernsey* direct from Jersey to Weymouth, after which the former Southern Railway veteran was dispatched to a lay-up berth in Southampton to await her fate.

Under the command of Captain Gerald Cartwright, the *Sarnia's* introductory cruise in the English Channel commenced from Southampton on 13th June, with press and invited guests being landed in Weymouth, and returning by train to Waterloo. Her first cross-Channel venture followed on 14th June, when she took a party of VIPs to Guernsey, and was joined by her sister, the *Caesarea* (on a scheduled visit), alongside the New Jetty in St. Peter Port Harbour.

It was a historic occasion for the island of Guernsey as the handsome new mail steamer *Sarnia*, dressed overall, entered St. Peter Port Harbour on the high tide at 08.00 on 14th June, and berthed at the New Jetty. She was greeted by siren blasts from the ships in port, and the signal 'Welcome' was flown from the Signal Station.

With almost perfect timing, the *Caesarea*, sister ship of the new *Sarnia*, and inbound from Jersey on a scheduled call, arrived at 10.25 with 524 passengers. As she entered port, she flew the *Sarnia's* signal letters and the message 'Welcome to the port'. The *Caesarea* left St. Peter Port for Weymouth at 11.20, having landed 236 passengers and embarked a further 400 for the Dorset port.

Despite the activity in the port, a small ceremony took place on board the *Sarnia*, in which Lady Arnold, the wife of the Bailiff of Guernsey, who had launched the ship in September 1960, presented Captain Cartwright, the ship's Master, with a painting as a gift from the people of the island.

The *Sarnia* entered commercial service, with her maiden revenue-earning voyage to the Channel Islands from Weymouth on 17th June 1961. This was the start of a marvellous partnership between those two ships which was to continue from Weymouth without major interruption (apart from winter relief work, mainly in the Dover Straits) for 12 years, until the appearance of the car ferry, *Falaise*, heralded the beginning of the end of classic passenger ferry operations between Weymouth and the Channel Islands. Indeed, a holiday in the Channel Islands from Weymouth commenced as soon as one climbed the gangway to board either the *Caesarea* or the *Sarnia*, such was the friendly atmosphere always to be found on those wonderful ferries.

All went well for the *Sarnia* throughout her first busy summer season in 1961, the first incident in which she was involved occurring during the winter period, when she hit the quay in St. Peter Port on 9th December, sustaining damage to the hull on the starboard side, which necessitated urgent repairs. Back in action in the New Year, the *Sarnia* paid her first visit to Folkestone in the spring, when she relieved the veteran steamer, *Canterbury*, from 12th to 17th April 1962.

A summer without incident followed, and on 19th November 1962, the *Sarnia* sailed to Dover to relieve the *Invicta* on the prestigious 'Golden Arrow' service to Calais. This was during the bitter winter of 1962/63, of course, when the *Sarnia* did not return to Weymouth until 30th January 1963. During her sojourn in the Straits of Dover, the *Sarnia* not only carried hundreds of passengers on their seasonal holidays, but huge quantities of mail as well, and it was on 12th December 1962 that she broke the record for the quantity of mail carried on that route, when she left Dover for Calais with 2,863 bags of Christmas mail.

On 23rd January 1967, the *Sarnia* was involved in an air/sea rescue operation whilst outward bound from the Channel Islands to Weymouth. At 11.00 on that morning, the British tanker *Constantia*, on a voyage from Amsterdam to Gibraltar with a cargo of fresh water, went aground on the Casquets some seven miles west of Alderney. Rough seas, whipped up by Force 6-8 winds pounded the crippled vessel, and the Captain gave orders for the 26-man crew to

The **Sarnia** dressed overall at St. Peter Port dressed overall for Jubilee Day in June 1977. *(Joe Ward)*

abandon ship. With a Shackleton aircraft co-ordinating the rescue operation, the Trinity House tender *Burhou* picked up 16 crew members from one of the ship's lifeboats, and landed them in Alderney, whilst the *Sarnia* plucked the ten remaining seamen from a life raft, and took them on to Weymouth, to complete her scheduled voyage without further delay.

In 1967, the new Passenger Terminal was completed at Weymouth Quay, and officially opened by the Mayor on 31st July. During that year, the Waterloo to Bournemouth railway line was electrified, speeding up timings of the trains and encouraging more people to travel to Weymouth by rail to catch the ferries to the Channel Islands. There were conspicuous increases in passenger numbers for both 1968 and 1969 as a result, and during her overhaul two years later, the *Sarnia* received considerable attention to her passenger accommodation similar to that carried out on the *Caesarea*.

The arrival in Weymouth of the *Falaise,* to open the brand new ro-ro service to Jersey in June 1973, whilst threatening the future of the conventional ferry programme did not affect the working

arrangements immediately, and they continued on the route as a pair, until the *Caesarea* completed her final scheduled voyage from the Channel Islands to Weymouth. It is worth recording that during that period, the *Sarnia* had the distinction of appearing as a design on one of the postage stamps in the States of Guernsey Mail Boat set, which was issued in 1973.

The normally reliable *Sarnia* had two fairly serious turbine problems during this period of operations, the first occurring on 28th June 1974, when she was withdrawn from service for ten days. The veteran steamer, *Maid of Orleans,* substituted for her making her second visit to Weymouth in as many years. When the *Sarnia* reported back for duty on 8th June, the *Maid of Orleans* was able to return to her normal sphere of operations in the Straits of Dover. Turbine trouble reared its ugly head again in April 1975 though, and on that occasion, the *Sarnia* was side-lined for two weeks whilst the problem was rectified. She returned to the Weymouth-Channel Isles link on 15th May 1975, to work the final summer with the *Caesarea*.

Following the departure of the *Caesarea* to Dover

in February 1976, the *Sarnia* carried on with her duties at Weymouth for another two summer seasons, and her activities certainly did not go unnoticed. On 23rd March 1976, the *Sarnia* was urgently required to convey over 200 stranded passengers from Weymouth to the Channel Islands, after the newly acquired car ferry, *Earl Godwin,* suffered serious generator problems for the third time in two weeks. The *Sarnia* later ran in tandem with the relief car ferry, *Normannia,* to transport hundreds of passengers, cars and freight vehicles between Weymouth and the Channel Islands in the absence of the *Earl Godwin,* and during an unusually heavily booked period at the end of March. The *Earl Godwin* did not return to duty until 6th April 1976.

The following year of 1977 was to be the final one for the *Sarnia* in British Railways ownership, and it proved to be a memorable one too, as it was most importantly, the Queen's Silver Jubilee Year. The 7th June was designated Jubilee Day, and for that auspicious occasion, 800 girl guides from all over Dorset chartered the *Sarnia* to take them on a day's outing from Weymouth to Guernsey.

The **Sarnia** with her sister the **Caesarea** were to be the main backbone of passenger operations until the era of the car ferry in the mid-sixties. *(Ferry Publications Library)*

On 28th June 1977, the *Sarnia* again brought much credit to her crew, and to Sealink (UK) Ltd. generally, when she attended the Queen's Silver Jubilee Review of the Fleet at Spithead, but sadly, the end of her life with British Railways was now in sight for the once proud Royal Mail Ship. Her master on that day was the ever popular Captain Colin Barker, who, unfortunately, didn't enjoy the best of health towards the end of his career.

The **Sarnia** swings in the harbour at St. Helier having just arrived at the port. *(Ambrose Greenway)*

The *Sarnia* completed her last regular voyage to the Channel Islands on Sunday 4th September 1977, and on the following Saturday (10th September), she made her final appearance on the route with another day trip to Guernsey, organised by the Ladies' Section of the Licensed Victuallers' Association. They made £2,400 for charity from the 1,100 happy passengers on board one of the most popular ships ever to set sail from Weymouth. The weather was fine, and under the command of Captain Gwyn Evans, the *Sarnia* gave a good account of herself as the sun set on her glorious years at Weymouth. Joe Ward, a chef on board the ship, and one of Sealink's best known photographers, was on hand to record the nostalgia of the final voyage. Dressed overall, and with the volunteer band of HMS *Heron*, Yeovilton, playing some stirring martial music, she arrived in St. Peter Port at 13.15.

There was great excitement in Guernsey as departure time approached, with passengers lining the ship's rail, and thousands of onlookers at various vantage points around St. Peter Port Harbour, waiting to witness the final departure of the *Sarnia.*

Then, at 18.30, the gangway was hoisted, the band struck up 'Land of Hope and Glory', and passengers threw streamers from ship to shore. As she drew away from the quay, there were three blasts for going astern, followed by longer blasts on her siren, and there was a chorus of farewells from yachts and other shipping in the harbour. She left St. Peter Port finally with the band playing 'Auld Lang Syne', and Captain Wolley, the local Harbour Master, sent a message to the master of the *Sarnia*, which read "Farewell to an old friend. Best wishes to you and all on board, from the Harbour Master and staff at St. Peter Port".

On her return to Weymouth from St. Peter Port, the *Sarnia* was de-stored and laid up for the winter months, pending a decision as to her future. And so ended 16 triumphant years on the Weymouth-Channel Islands route, a period when the *Caesarea* and *Sarnia* ruled the waves in the Western Channel, and were rarely out of commission, except for annual inspections, refurbishment work and minor mishaps. It seems incredible, too, that the elegant *Sarnia* had transported over 3 million happy

The **Sarnia** dressed overall at the Silver Jubilee Review in the Solent. *(Ambrose Greenway)*

passengers between Weymouth and the Channel Islands, during her impressive career with British Railways.

Put up for sale in the spring of 1978, the *Sarnia* was purchased in the April by Supasave Supermarkets (Midland) Ltd., a Guernsey registered company, for operation by Channel Cruise Lines as a cruising vessel between Ostend and Dunkirk, with shopping facilities for Belgian and French tourists. The ferry finally left Weymouth on 24th May 1978, bound for Immingham, where she was converted into a floating supermarket, with shopping arcades selling everything from the traditional duty free wines, spirits and tobacco goods, to clothing, photographic material and electrical items. Renamed *Aquamart,* she was set to open the duty free shopping service between Ostend and Dunkirk on 24th July 1978, apparently with the approval of the Belgian and French Customs authorities. Ten days before the enterprise was due to get underway, however, the French authorities announced that taxes would be charged on all goods being landed with an import value exceeding FFr.140, and two days before sailing, the Belgians followed suit, applying additional tax to certain goods such as spirits, cigarettes and electrical equipment.

The 800 passengers who sailed on the inaugural voyage, and those who travelled on the subsequent cruises, were advised of the new taxation plans, and as a result, travellers were quick to abandon the *Aquamart,* with only 100 passengers departing on the Saturday morning (29th July) sailing, at the end of a very frustrating week. Unfortunately, Channel Cruise Line failed to persuade the French and Belgian authorities to modify their taxation demands for day trippers so the service was suspended, and on 4th August 1978, the *Aquamart* was dispatched to the West India Dock in London to await a decision as to its future, which now looked very uncertain.

She remained in London for several months, and was finally sold to Greek interests in December 1978. Renamed *Golden Star,* she left the River Thames under tow by the Dutch tug *Groenland* on 20th January 1979, bound for Piraeus, where, on arrival, she entered the Greek domestic trade, where she

remained for just two years before being sold on again, this time to Saudi Arabian owners, Hitta Establishment of Jeddah. Her name was changed yet again and she became the *Saudi Golden Star,* being employed on a Middle East service carrying pilgrims between Port Said and Jeddah.

After serving on that route for quite some time, her general condition inevitably deteriorated, she was withdrawn and laid up in the mid 1980s, and never steamed again. Sold eventually to Pakistani ship breakers, the former celebrated *Sarnia* passed quietly into history, when she was towed to Gadani Beach and put to the torch in 1987.

CALEDONIAN PRINCESS

The *Caledonian Princess* was built for the Stranraer-Larne route at a total cost of £1.85 million and operated her maiden voyage on 16th December 1961. The *Caledonian Princess,* or 'Caley P' as she was to be affectionately known throughout her long career, was a stern-loading car ferry with a gross tonnage of 3,630. Her main dimensions were 353 feet in length, with a breadth of 57 feet and a draught of 12 feet. A twin screw steamship, she was powered by two DR geared Denny turbines with oil-fired boilers, which gave her a very comfortable cruising speed of 20 knots. She was the first railway boat to be fitted with Denny-Brown AEG folding stabilisers, and another important feature of the ship was the Voith-Schneider lateral thrust unit at the bow.

The *Caledonian Princess* was given a certificate for 1,400 passengers who were accommodated in two classes, with 400 in first class and 1,000 in the second. Cabin accommodation for the passengers consisted of 82 first class berths, comprising 2 two berth cabins-de-luxe with the remainder in one and two berth cabins. Second class passengers had a choice of the 94 berths in two and four berth cabins.

The public rooms were spacious and comfortable, with a first class restaurant seating 50 persons, and a second class cafeteria with 140 seats, both situated on the promenade deck, together with the first and second class smoke rooms. The first and second class lounges with bars were to be found on the boat deck.

The **Caledonian Princess** prepares to leave the berth for Guernsey. *(Miles Cowsill)*

The main car deck of the *Caledonian Princess* had spaces for 103 motor cars and a total of 29 trailers could also be carried, but with a consequential reduction in the number of cars. A 22 feet diameter turntable, which was operated electronically, was positioned at the after end of the ship to enable vehicles to be turned before stowage.

With the growth in traffic on the North Channel, a new ship was ordered (the *Antrim Princess),* and the plan was for her to run opposite the *Caledonian Princess* throughout the summer months, with the new arrival remaining on the route all year round, and the now well-established *Caledonian Princess* used as the winter relief ship to cover all eventualities, including annual overhauls.

Following a period in service at Fishguard, she left the St George's Channel link at the end of June 1975, and departed for Weymouth, where she commenced service on 15th July. She remained on the Weymouth payroll until 31st January 1976, when British Railways decided that she would partner the *Earl Godwin* on the multi-purpose operation between the Dorset port

and the Channel Islands, for which the *Caledonian Princess* would require refitting and conversion into a one class ship.

Early in February 1976, the *Caledonian Princess* left Weymouth for Immingham, where the necessary work was to be undertaken at a cost of £426,000 to provide the maximum number of reclining seats for night travellers, and to improve other passenger facilities. The work was initially centred around the boat deck, where the existing entrance lounge and stewardesses' accommodation at the after end were removed, and replaced by a new stairway enclosure, smart ladies' and gents' toilets, and a first aid room.

The after end of the open deck was converted into an additional lounge with 116 seats, and a rearrangement of the deck's forward lounge provided an extra 88 seats. On the promenade deck, the old second class smoke room and baggage room were reconstructed to form a new lounge extending to the ship's sides, and cabin and toilet facilities were provided for female staff, by adapting existing passenger cabins on the port side. Two new shops were sited forward of the midship's lounge, and a new tea bar built in the old bureau area. The upper deck wasn't forgotten either, the port side of the old second class cafeteria being converted into a television lounge, and extra seats placed in the former first class dining saloon. In fact, a total of 570 additional seats were installed throughout the ship, and all were vinyl covered.

On completion of the work, the *Caledonian Princess* sailed for Weymouth, and took up service on the Channel Islands' route on 12th May 1976, remaining on the link until 14th December, when she was dispatched to Holyhead on relief duty. In fact, she was taken to the Welsh port by a Holyhead crew, and Captain John Attwood acted as the Weymouth pilot to allow the vessel to leave port. The *Caledonian Princess* was back in Weymouth early in March 1977, and entered employment on the Channel Isles' programme, running opposite to the *Earl Godwin* throughout the summer period.

Sealink opened a brand new service from Portsmouth to the Channel Islands at the end of that year, an act that was to have serious repercussions for Weymouth within a relatively short space of time. Even the opening day affected Weymouth, due to the fact that the newly acquired *Earl William* was not available to inaugurate the service in November 1977, and Weymouth's very own *Earl Godwin* was pressed into action at Portsmouth, with the *Caledonian Princess* being required to delay her winter overhaul, in order to maintain the Channel Islands' service from the Dorset port.

Fears were expressed at Weymouth regarding the Portsmouth venture, and there was such serious disagreement between British Railways' management and the National Union of Seamen over manning levels and unresolved wage negotiations appertaining to the new service, that a strike was called on the ferries operating routes to the Channel Islands from 31st October 1977. The last sailing from Weymouth was the night service on Friday/Saturday 28/29th October, operated by the *Caledonian Princess*, and when the *Earl Godwin* arrived in Weymouth during the afternoon of Saturday 29th October, she 'sat' on the ramp over

the weekend. In actual fact, she was due to inaugurate the Portsmouth service on 1st November, but the arrangements were suspended. Following a ballot of members, agreement was reached, and the industrial action was eventually called off, but the situation didn't really get back to normal until 8th November 1977, when the *Earl Godwin* opened the Portsmouth-Channel Isles route, leaving the *Caledonian Princess* to handle the Weymouth traffic.

There was more disruption during the following weekend, when hundreds of tourists were delayed by severe gales in the English Channel, and at one stage, both the *Caledonian Princess* and the *Earl Godwin* were stormbound in St. Peter Port Harbour, the very first occasion on which they had been seen together in Guernsey. The *Caledonian Princess* had arrived from Weymouth at 11.40 on Saturday 12th November 1977, which was five hours late, with 850 passengers on board, 622 of them due to disembark in Jersey. Because of the Force 9 wind, the ferry remained at the New Jetty until 08.00 on 13th November, and all those passengers for Jersey were made as comfortable as possible on board.

The *Earl Godwin*, outward bound from Portsmouth to Jersey and then Guernsey, battled through atrocious weather conditions at reduced speed. Her Master, Captain Paul Baker, decided to make for Guernsey first, and dropped anchor off St. Peter Port after ten hours at sea. The ferry rolled badly at anchor, making life almost intolerable for the 289 passengers on board, only 22 of whom were due to land in St. Peter Port. There was also concern about the movement of a freight unit on the car deck, but crew members reacted swiftly to secure it, and a potentially nasty situation was averted.

At 18.00 on 12th November 1977, the *Earl Godwin* entered port and tied up alongside the container berth to land her Guernsey passengers, and at the same time, transfer her Jersey-bound passengers to the *Caledonian Princess* before going to anchor again. The *Caledonian Princess* set off for Jersey at 08.00 on the following day, but conditions were still extremely bad, and she had to ride out the storm off St. Helier until late afternoon. Shortly after the *Caledonian*

An outstanding view of the Denny-built ship **Caledonian Princess** at full speed outward bound from St. Helier for Weymouth.

(Kevin Le Scelleur)

Princess left St. Peter Port, the *Earl Godwin* re-entered harbour and discharged her vehicles at the ramp, after which she departed for Jersey at noon, with a few breakaway passengers, and vehicles for discharge in St. Helier.

During the following week, the Channel Islands' services returned to normal, but the *Earl William* didn't pick up the Portsmouth timetable until 16th January 1978, and the *Earl Godwin* returned to its home base in Weymouth, allowing the *Caledonian Princess* to proceed to Newhaven to relieve the *Earl Leofric* on the Dieppe link. This relief job was to give British Railways' management quite a headache, because the *Earl Godwin*, left alone on the Weymouth-Channel Isles working, also had to delay her annual overhaul until the return of the *Caledonian Princess*. When she (*Earl Godwin*) eventually went to the yard, she became involved in an industrial dispute, which further delayed her completion and return to duty. As a result, Sealink had to charter the *Viking Victory* from Thoresen Car Ferries A/S, to join the *Caledonian Princess* on the

multi-purpose service from Weymouth to the Channel Islands, the chartered vessel being employed from 3rd to 26th March 1978.

For the Royal Visit to Guernsey on 28th June 1978, a 'Princess' dressed overall, provided the backdrop for Her Majesty the Queen and the Duke of Edinburgh, when they came ashore from the Royal Yacht *Britannia,* which lay at anchor off St. Peter Port. It was Sealink's own *Caledonian Princess* operating the 08.00 Jersey to Guernsey and Weymouth sailing, and under the command of Captain John Davies she led a chorus of ships' sirens to mark the arrival of the Royal party.

In January 1979, Weymouth was closed to Channel Islands' ro-ro traffic for five weeks. Since the *Caledonian Princess* was off service at refit, British Railways decided to send the *Earl Godwin* to work the Portsmouth-Channel Islands route in place of the *Earl William*, which was undergoing damage repairs in a shipyard in Falmouth. Despite local protests, the transfer of the *Earl Godwin* went ahead, leaving Weymouth staff

The **Caledonian Princess** at the linkspan at Weymouth having just arrived from the Channel Islands. *(Ferry Publications Library)*

frustrated and idle during that late winter period.

With the return to duty of the *Caledonian Princess*, Sealink announced the end of the temporary cessation of the Weymouth-Channel Islands services as from 1st March 1979. The *Caledonian Princess* was due to re-open the link at the regular departure time of 13.30, but unfortunately she didn't arrive in Weymouth until 13.00, and the members of her crew and port workers involved, did extremely well to ensure that the 200 booked passengers, 75 motor cars and extra stores were loaded without any further delay. This enabled the ferry to leave Weymouth at 15.25, just under two hours late.

Early in May 1980, Portsmouth's *Earl William* suffered generator trouble, and was withdrawn from service for urgent repairs. The *Caledonian Princess* sailed from Weymouth on 4th May, and took over the Portsmouth-Channel Islands timetable on the following day, pending the arrival of Townsend Thoresen's ferry *Free Enterprise II,* which had been hastily chartered by Sealink. However, due to her inability to carry freight, this chartered vessel was found to be most unsuitable for the Portsmouth-Channel Islands working and she was switched to Weymouth, where she was found to be equally unsuitable, in exchange for the very adaptable *Earl Godwin,* a move that again indicated that Weymouth was becoming a second class port as far as British Railways/Sealink were concerned. The *Caledonian Princess* and the *Free Enterprise II* worked the Weymouth-Channel Isles route from 21st May to 11th June 1980, when the *Earl William* returned to duty at Portsmouth, enabling the *Earl Godwin* to rejoin the *Caledonian Princess* at Weymouth at the expense of the 'FE II', which was returned to her owners.

The ubiquitous *Caledonian Princess* made many friends during her long career with the Caledonian Steam Packet Company, British Railways and Sealink, particularly on the North Channel link in the early days, and also during her five-year spell on the Weymouth payroll between 1976 and 1981, when she steamed over 120,000 miles. But the year 1981 dawned with the knowledge that it was likely to be the last one in British Railways' ownership for the *Caledonian Princess*, and it was with more than a

tinge of sadness that we bid her farewell from Weymouth.

Her last arrival in the Dorset port from the Channel Islands was scheduled for Saturday 2nd May 1981, and indeed, the local paper reported her arrival that day as the end of her final voyage from the Channel Islands. The *Caledonian Princess* left Weymouth almost immediately for Avonmouth, where she was overhauled before proceeding to Dover on 28th May, as a direct replacement for the former Weymouth-Channel Islands passenger steamer, *Caesarea,* which had been sold. The *Earl William,* just relieved by the newly acquired *Earl Granville* on the Portsmouth station, was transferred to Weymouth, to replace the *Caledonian Princess.*

The *Caledonian Princess* remained on the Dover Strait until 26th September 1981, when she made her final, and Dover's last steam powered, cross-Channel voyage. She was withdrawn from service and sailed to Newhaven to lay up pending disposal. She then remained tied up in Newhaven for over a year, being finally purchased by the Quadrini Group, a Newcastle entertainment organisation, who planned to use her as a floating restaurant and nightclub on the River Tyne. After a period of time on the Tyne and then Glasgow she returned again to Newcastle. She was sold to Greek interests for scrap in 2008 and sailed for Aliaga in July for the breaker's yard.

SVEA DROTT/ EARL GODWIN

The *Earl Godwin* will forever be remembered as Weymouth's longest serving car ferry, and arguably the most popular completing almost 15 years of loyal service from the Dorset port. However it was as the Swedish charter vessel, *Svea Drott*, that she first appeared on the scene in August 1974. She had been hastily scrambled from her lay-up berth in Oskarshamn, Sweden, to assist British Railways in their hour of need, when the *Falaise* was withdrawn from operations.

Facing enormous difficulties in procuring a suitable relief vessel to cover the packed late summer programme on the Weymouth-Channel Islands route, British Railways' management were extremely lucky to find the Swedish car ferry, *Svea*

The **Earl Godwin** on passage to Weymouth off Portland Bill. *(Ambrose Greenway)*

Drott, available, and she was chartered immediately. She instantly warmed up her engines for the long trip to Weymouth, where she arrived and entered service on 19th August 1974.

The *Svea Drott* had been constructed by Oresundsvarvet AB in Landskrona, Sweden, to the order of Stockholms Rederi AB Svea, and was launched on 20th January 1966. She was delivered to her owners on 8th June 1966, and sailed on her maiden voyage from Helsingborg to Travemunde via Copenhagen two days later.

The *Svea Drott* was 99 metres long, 18.3 metres in breadth and she had a draught of 4.6 metres. Her gross tonnage was 4,018 tonnes. Her machinery consisted of two 12 cylinder Klockner-Humboldt-Deutz diesel engines, and two 6 cylinder engines, both types being four stroke, single acting and turbo charged, with one of each type coupled to a twin engine reduction gear with hydraulic couplings. Two Kamewa hydraulically operated controllable pitch propellers helped to push her through the water at a comfortable 20 knots, although she never achieved this speed in her later career as the *Earl Godwin*, 17.5

to 18 knots being the maximum her Chief Engineer could coax out of her.

Her navigational equipment consisted of the most up-to-date Sperry gyro compass, direction finder and Kelvin Hughes echo sounder and radar unit, and she was fitted with Kamewa bow thrusters. Life saving gear included 1,100 life belts, 25 life buoys, 27 auto inflating life rafts, each of which could hold 25 persons, two 27 feet glass fibre motor boats capable of carrying 66 survivors each, and four 27 feet rowing boats each with a capacity of 63 souls.

The *Svea Drott* had a certificate to carry 928 passengers, with sleeping accommodation for about 200 in berths on two of the passenger decks. On the saloon deck there were five double cabins, two for three persons and 25 able to take four weary travellers, whilst on the lower deck there were 11 double cabins, eight for four persons and four large cabins capable of sleeping up to eight members of a family.

To provide much needed sustenance for passengers, there were two spacious dining saloons, the larger one on the boat deck seating 165, and the slightly smaller one on the saloon deck able to handle 118 passengers at one sitting. On the boat deck there was also a very comfortable lounge known as the Siesta Saloon, which had seats for 108 voyagers, and the main bar, stocked with a variety of drinks, was situated on the saloon deck. Apart from passengers, the *Svea Drott* could carry up to 185 motor cars, depending on length, and her extensive vehicle deck could accommodate 17 high-sided lorries, or a mixture of both cars and lorries.

Initially, the *Svea Drott* was chartered by the British nationalised concern for 35 days and entered the Channel Islands' service on 19th August 1974. She was only eight years old when she was taken on charter terms, and British Railways soon became enamoured with her, despite her obvious limitations at that time. These were mainly due to the lack of stabilisers.

British Railways' management liked the *Svea Drott*, and this was a sentiment also shared by her crew and many of her passengers alike, so it was felt that the problems could be eradicated without too much difficulty. In fact, British Railways' enthusiasm for the attractive ferry never waned, and within three months she had been purchased by Lloyds Leasing of London for 23 million Swedish Kronors, and she was handed over to British Railways on long-term lease, at Helsingborg on 10th January 1975. The *Svea Drott* was renamed *Earl Godwin*, which was in keeping with British Railways' policy at that time of naming their vessels after the noblemen of England. Earl Godwin

was, in fact, the Earl of Wessex, whose son, Harold, later became the King of England.

A skeleton crew under the command of Captain John MacMillan, with Gwyn Evans as Chief Officer and Danny Ridout as Boatswain, travelled to Helsingborg from Weymouth to collect the ship and it took the Weymouth team three days to make her ready for sea. She left Helsingborg on 13th January 1975, but encountered heavy seas in the Skagerrak, in which problems developed with the starboard anchor chains resulting from a rusty flute. The vessel had to heave to in atrocious conditions whilst the deck crew remedied the situation.

The *Earl Godwin* arrived at Harwich on 14th January, where her two main engines were dismantled and dispatched to Cologne for machining and rebedding. The ferry was then taken around to the British Railways' Marine Workshops at Holyhead, where she was to remain for a year whilst the biggest conversion job ever tackled by those workshops was carried out.

Much of the work was performed on the passenger accommodation, where the saloon deck was completely gutted, all the cabins removed and the whole area converted into large open passenger lounges with aircraft style seating. A new cafeteria was also constructed on the saloon deck, with the galley being redesigned and refitted. Extra aircraft style seating was installed on the boat deck, too, in a newly appointed lounge area for weary passengers. The only cabins remaining after the major

The ***Earl Godwin*** arrives at St. Peter Port in the brilliant sunshine from Jersey. *(Ambrose Greenway)*

The ***Earl Godwin*** departs from Guernsey with a full load of passengers for Weymouth. *(Ambrose Greenway)*

An afternoon scene at Weymouth in June 1984 sees the **Earl Godwin** going astern from the Dorset port outward bound for Jersey. *(Miles Cowsill)*

reconstruction work was completed, were 16 situated under the car deck, and lack of genuine sleeping accommodation on the overnight run between Weymouth and the Channel Islands was, arguably, the only deficiency in an otherwise superbly presented ferry.

The ship's air conditioning system was completely modernised, and most important of all, a new bow door was installed and stabilisers fitted, to ensure every comfort combined with safety, for passengers when on passage in inclement weather. However her reconstruction took longer than expected, and it was not until February 1976 that the *Earl Godwin* was ready for her new employment on the Weymouth-Channel Isles route, her main engines having been returned by road from Cologne, and refitted at Holyhead.

Entering the Channel Islands' service for the first time as *Earl Godwin*, she made a little history by being the first ferry during the 20th century to commence her maiden voyage the 'wrong way' from the Channel Islands into Weymouth, a trip that she undertook on 2nd February 1976. Her arrival on the

Weymouth stage marked the beginning of Sealink's multi-purpose service between the Dorset port and the Channel Islands, in which her running mate was to be the ubiquitous *Caledonian Princess*, the ever faithful passenger steamer *Sarnia* being retained, to provide additional sailings and excursions during the high season. The summer timetable for the two car ferries remained virtually unchanged for several years, with the *Earl Godwin* offering an afternoon departure from Weymouth at 13.30, and the *Caledonian Princess* a late evening one.

The service became extremely popular with the travelling public, although the *Earl Godwin's* first season was marred by generator problems, and on 23rd March 1976, she had to be withdrawn from service, after engineers had worked around the clock in an attempt to cure her ills. It was the third fault in two weeks, and when taken out of service, she remained idle for almost a fortnight as spare parts were awaited from West Germany. With the locally based *Caledonian Princess* unavailable, the *Normannia* was selected for the relief job, arriving from Newhaven to pick up the timetable on 26th

March, and transport 110 cars, out of a backlog of 150 vehicles that had built up on the quay at Weymouth, to the Channel Islands. Meanwhile the faithful *Sarnia* plucked hundreds of booked passengers off the quay at Weymouth, and worked in tandem with the *Normannia* until the *Earl Godwin* was restored to duty. Unfortunately, the Channel Isles' service was hit by a dockers' strike in Jersey on 29th March, which lasted a week. No vehicles were landed in St. Helier, and the end of the industrial action virtually coincided with the *Earl Godwin's* return to duty on 6th April 1976.

The *Earl Godwin* opened the new Portsmouth-Channel Islands service on 8th November 1977, until 16th January 1978, when the *Earl William* entered service. For the next couple of years, both Weymouth and Portsmouth services operated side by side with very little trouble. In March 1981, the *Earl Godwin* was sent to the Isle of Man to cover the Douglas-Heysham service. Some two years later in mid-January 1983, the Channel Islands' programme was badly affected by the weather. On 14th January the *Earl Godwin* reached Jersey from Weymouth some 2½ hours late, and found Portsmouth's *Earl Granville* occupying the only ramp. The *Earl Godwin* was sent to the old mail boat berth at St. Helier to land her passengers, and, following the departure of the *Earl Granville*, the *Earl Godwin* was able to reposition to the ro-ro berth, to discharge her motor cars and freight vehicles.

The *Earl Godwin* was relieved on the Channel Isles' route on 18th January by the *Earl William's* return from dry docking and repairs at Falmouth, and she then went to Barry for an extensive refit. She didn't return to Weymouth until 28th February, when she picked up the night service to the Channel Islands with the 22.30 departure on 1st March 1983.

The *Earl Godwin's* first major accident occurred on 15th October 1984, when, in thick fog, she ran aground on rocks east of Elizabeth Castle near St. Helier. There were 240 passengers on board the ferry at the time, and everyone was called to boat stations and instructed to put on life jackets. Although the ship was not in any immediate danger, the Master requested the assistance of the States of Jersey tug,

Duke of Normandy, and ordered that all lifeboats be prepared for lowering. In the event, the tug was able to tow the *Earl Godwin* off the rocks, and the ferry was able to make it into port at St. Helier under her own power, where divers made an early inspection and found damage below the waterline. Temporary repairs were carried out before the *Earl Godwin* sailed to Holyhead for dry docking and permanent repairs, her annual refit being brought forward to run concurrently with the repair programme.

Regrettably, the *Earl Godwin's* winter programme had to be cancelled and passengers due to travel on the scheduled services from Weymouth to the Channel Islands, or vice versa, suffered the slight inconvenience of having to rearrange their bookings and travel on the *Earl William.*

During the winter of 1984/85, plans had been formulated to introduce new sailing programmes to the Channel Islands from Portsmouth and Weymouth. These were to be known as the 'Starliner' and 'Sunliner' services, the former being night voyages from Portsmouth, as the name implied, with day runs from Weymouth under the 'Sunliner' banner, in which the *Earl Godwin* and the *Earl Harold* (the former *Ailsa Princess,* renamed *Earl Harold* on 24th May 1985) were to figure prominently.

When the *Earl Godwin* returned to Weymouth from Holyhead in December 1984, she berthed alongside the Cargo Stage, where repainting of the ship in the new Sealink British Ferries livery was put in hand by the local crew. On 31st March 1985 she opened the new summer programme with a 15.15 departure from Weymouth, although the 'Sunliner' service did not become fully operational until 24th May 1985, when the *Earl Godwin* was joined by the recently renamed and refurbished *Earl Harold.*

Unfortunately, the new services from Portsmouth and Weymouth were a disaster from the outset, trade figures from Portsmouth being far worse than those at the Dorset port. The 'Sunliner' service at Weymouth was a little more successful, as fares on that route were similar to those offered by Channel Island Ferries at Portsmouth, but there was still a combined deficit of some £6 million on both Sealink British Ferries' services at the end of the trading season.

For the week commencing 17th February 1986, all services at Weymouth were suspended. The *Earl Godwin* was still undergoing refurbishment work on the Clyde, and the *Earl William,* her relief at Weymouth, was required back in Portsmouth to cover the absence of the *Earl Granville,* as the latter had been sent to the Pool of London on a promotional exercise. So the Channel Islands' service from Weymouth was closed down for a week, with all arrivals and sailings from and to the islands being transferred to Portsmouth. Once again the Dorset port was in the firing line, which prompted heavy criticism from the Mayor of Weymouth & Portland who called the latest treatment of Weymouth "shabby and disastrous".

The *Earl Harold* was drafted in to re-open the Weymouth-Channel Isles route on Monday 24th February 1986, and remained on the link until the *Earl Godwin* returned from refit on 3rd March. The latter vessel continued on the Channel Islands' working until 26th March 1986, when she was assigned for duty on the summer route between Weymouth and Cherbourg, with the *Earl Harold* reverting to the Channel Islands' service as the sole ferry on the route.

The *Earl Godwin* had only been in action for five days, when she broke down in Cherbourg with steering gear trouble on Easter Monday 31st March 1986. She was off service for two days, and passengers had to be diverted to the Portsmouth route. Fortunately, the *Earl Godwin* was back in action, to handle some heavy seasonal bookings, on 2nd April 1986.

As the summer of 1986 progressed, however, it became increasingly apparent that Sealink British Ferries were losing ground to Channel Island Ferries at Portsmouth, and whilst the Weymouth services to the Channel Islands and Cherbourg were carrying reasonable loads, with the *Earl Godwin's* voyages to Cherbourg being particularly well supported, the South Coast ports would be facing an enormous deficit at the end of the summer season.

On 30th September 1986, Sealink British Ferries announced a suspension of the Channel Islands' services, with complete closure at Weymouth, which resulted in industrial action on a huge scale, with ferry crews involved in 'sit in' strikes, particularly in Weymouth, where the *Earl Godwin* was on the ramp. The 'sit in' on board the *Earl Godwin* lasted for four weeks. The *Earl Godwin* remained at Weymouth until 27th March 1987, when she was dispatched to the River Fal to lay up for an indefinite period. She was actually taken to Falmouth by the same crew responsible for the delivery of the *Earl William* to the Fal three days previously. The *Earl Godwin* remained at her Cornish lay-up berth for almost a year, before being dry docked and overhauled in Falmouth prior to opening the seasonal route between Weymouth and Cherbourg on 17th March 1988, but due to problems with her bow thrust unit, she did not arrive in Weymouth until two hours before departure time on that day.

The *Earl Godwin* remained on the Weymouth-Cherbourg service for two months, her last day on the route being 25th May 1988. She was replaced by the *Earl Harold* and on 26th May she proceeded to Southampton, where she lay temporarily, before going on to Portsmouth to join the *Earl Granville* on the Cherbourg link from that port. At the end of a fairly busy season, the *Earl Godwin* was dispatched once again to her lay-up berth on the Fal on 14th October 1988.

On 3rd January 1989, the *Earl Godwin* returned to the fray, running a freight only service to the Channel Islands from Portsmouth on charter to Mainland Market Deliveries (MMD), and this employment continued for several weeks. Following completion of the charter work at Portsmouth, the *Earl Godwin* returned to Weymouth, and opened the seasonal Cherbourg service on 22nd March 1989.

The *Earl Godwin* was involved in an extremely interesting working during August 1989. The *Earl Granville,* whilst operating the Portsmouth-Cherbourg service, hit an underwater obstruction in the French port on 19th August. She was withdrawn for major repairs, and the Portsmouth-Cherbourg link closed temporarily, leaving the *Earl Godwin* at Weymouth to cope with the build up of vehicles in Cherbourg. The *Skarvoy,* was chartered to run in tandem with the *Earl Godwin,* but while the visiting Norwegian ferry

The late evening sunshine catches the **Earl Godwin** on the 'Sunliner' service outward bound from St. Helier. *(Miles Cowsill)*

had excellent car carrying capabilities, she did not possess a certificate or facilities for passengers.

With a single linkspan in Weymouth, and the *Earl Godwin* packed with passengers, many of whom had their motor cars on board the *Skarvoy*, this meant that the *Skarvoy* had to wait for the *Earl Godwin* to relinquish its position on the ramp before it could discharge its cargo of vehicles.

The Isle of Man Steamship Company's ferry, *Mona's Queen,* was chartered to re-open the Portsmouth-Cherbourg link on 4th September 1989, but she was a side-loading vessel and problems were encountered at Portsmouth. As a result, the *Earl Godwin* switched to Portsmouth for a short period in exchange for the *Mona's Queen*. Later, on 15th September, the *St. Patrick II* was chartered from Irish Continental, and she remained on the Portsmouth station until relieved by the *Earl Godwin,* following closure of the Weymouth-Cherbourg summer service early in October.

For seven weeks from 1st November 1989, the *Earl Godwin* worked a freight only service between Portsmouth and Cherbourg. This employment

terminated on 23rd December, and the *Earl Godwin* was withdrawn from service and dispatched to Weymouth, where she arrived on Christmas Eve to lay up pending disposal. Seen by representatives of the Italian shipping company, NaVarMa, she was purchased by that company in February 1990 and subsequently renamed *Moby Baby*. Sea trials were arranged by the new owners, found to be quite satisfactory, and the *Moby Baby* finally departed from Weymouth on 30th March 1990, bringing to an end 130 years of railway shipping at the port. She remains in service today operating between the Italian mainland and the island of Elba.

EARL GRANVILLE

Between 1970 and 1974, six almost identical car ferries were built for the Viking Line of Finland by the Jos. L. Meyer shipyard at Papenburg in West Germany. The first of these sisters to operate on the English Channel was the *Earl Granville.* She was launched at Meyer's yard in Papenburg as the *Viking 4* on 16th March 1973 and entered service on Viking Line's Stockholm-Mariehamn-Turku route exactly

The *Earl Granville* undergoing part of her overhaul at Weymouth. The marine staff at the port were responsible for many years for looking after the ships serving the Channel Islands. *(Dave Habgood)*

three months later on 16th June. By 1980, however, the Viking Line was expanding and investing in larger ships, and the *Viking 4* was found to be surplus to requirements. So she was laid up in Mariehamn, and offered for sale.

She immediately attracted the attention of Sealink (UK) Ltd., who were looking for a new acquisition for their Channel Islands' services, and so Senior Master, Captain Paul Baker and Chief Engineer Ron Flood flew to Mariehamn to view the ship. After a satisfactory visual check, the ferry was sent to Bremerhaven for dry-docking and further examination, during which the hull was repainted. New Denny-Brown stabilisers were despatched to the yard in Bremerhaven, and fitted before the *Viking 4* left the port for her builder's yard in Papenburg, where further work was undertaken. The vessel was purchased by Williams & Glynn Industrial Leasing Company Ltd. on behalf of Sealink on 25th August 1980, and she was renamed *Earl Granville*, prior to being sent for refit to Meyer's at Papenburg where work included the installation of new Crossley-Pielstick engines and gearboxes. The sleeping arrangements were reduced from 280 to 195 berths in a total of 90 single, two berth and four berth cabins but to compensate for that reduction, over 600 reclining sleeping chairs were provided on D-deck, where the cafeteria and fan club were originally sited. Some cabins were also removed from C-deck to provide even more reclining seats for passengers' use and a special Conference Room was constructed and could seat 36 persons. This was a

'first' for a Sealink ferry, and the room could be doubled up to accommodate private parties on board, as well as for meetings and conferences.

With refit satisfactorily completed, the *Earl Granville* was delivered to Portsmouth in March 1981 and sailed on her inaugural familiarisation trip on 26th March. She made her maiden voyage three days later on the 23.00 sailing to the islands, becoming the company's flagship for the Channel Island fleet.

Her first two months on the Portsmouth-Channel Islands link were uneventful but unfortunately she was beset with a number of problems in June 1981. Firstly on 10th June, when outward bound to the Channel Isles from Portsmouth with 100 passengers and cars, a generator failed and the *Earl Granville* had to drop anchor for several hours whilst repairs were carried out. This resulted in the ferry being six hours late on arrival in Jersey. Three days later, engine trouble caused considerable delay, with the ship arriving in St. Helier on one engine, and the normal call at St. Peter Port in Guernsey cancelled as a result.

A much more serious incident was to follow on 22nd June 1981 when a fire was discovered in a domestic boiler three hours after departure from the port at 23.00 and this was to cause over £200,000 worth of damage to the central heating system and other important pieces of electrical equipment in the ship. As her Master, Captain Tom Bill, said at the time, "It isn't much fun to be awakened in the middle of the night and told that your ship is on fire." The *Earl Granville* limped back to Portsmouth, where she arrived at 05.00, and her 360 passengers and their cars were offloaded safely. After breakfast, they set off for Weymouth to pick up the afternoon sailing by the *Earl Godwin* to the Channel Islands and the *Earl Granville* was despatched immediately to Husband's shipyard in Southampton where she lay for three weeks undergoing urgent repairs. The Portsmouth-Channel Isles service was suspended for three days until the *Caledonian Princess* arrived from Dover to relieve the stricken vessel, although in actual fact, she shared the programme with the *Earl William*.

The *Earl Granville* did not return to duty until 17th July and the next day she was in more trouble when she hit the ramp in St. Helier. This caused

The clean and modern lines of the *Earl Granville* outward bound from St. Helier during her first year in service with Sealink. (*Ambrose Greenway*)

damage to the linkspan which required urgent attention over several days necessitating the use of cranes to offload the ferry's vehicles, the other ramp in St. Helier being occupied by the Emeraude ferry *Solidor*. Tidal conditions forced the *Earl Granville* to proceed to Guernsey to pick up passengers and cars for Portsmouth and on her return to Jersey, a small fire broke out in lagging surrounding some pipework. This was quickly extinguished, but the ship was further delayed, whilst the authorities in St. Helier carried out safety inspections. She finally departed during the evening, arriving in Portsmouth several hours adrift. Temporary repairs to the linkspan in St. Helier brought it back into use within a week, with a more permanent job being completed during the following winter period.

The *Earl Granville's* troubled first season with Sealink was virtually brought to a close on 9th October 1981 when she ran into a fierce storm off the Isle of Wight in which 12 passengers and a stewardess received injuries that required hospital treatment as soon as the vessel docked. In addition, over 60 cars were damaged after breaking loose on the car deck in heavy seas.

Her 1982 programme was virtually free of problems, except for the appalling weather conditions encountered in late September of that year. On 16th December 1982, the *Earl Granville* made her first visit to Weymouth, when she arrived for ramp trials following proposals to introduce an 'Extended Service' during the summer of 1983, designed to take in Weymouth, Portsmouth, the Channel Islands and Cherbourg in round trips during the busiest weekends at the height of the summer season. The trials were satisfactory but the visit heralded another spell of bad weather, particularly in January 1983. Heavy seas caused much damage to the bow visor of the *Earl Granville* on 20th January, and her sailing from Portsmouth to the Channel Islands on the following day had to be cancelled, in order to carry out repairs.

The *Earl Granville* made her first departure from Weymouth with passengers and cars, on Saturday 2nd July 1983, the opening day of the new 'Extended Service', in which the regular Weymouth-Channel Isles and Weymouth-Cherbourg sailings

Sealink purchased the **Earl Granville** from Viking Line to boost their Portsmouth-Channel Islands operation. *(Kevin Le Scelleur)*

were supplemented by weekend visits from the Portsmouth-based ferry.

The *Earl Granville's* routine was a departure from Portsmouth at 23.00 on the Friday, arriving first in Jersey and then on to Guernsey during Saturday morning, leaving St. Peter Port for Weymouth at 10.25 for a booked arrival in the Dorset port at 14.30, before leaving Weymouth for Cherbourg at 15.30 after a quick turnaround. Arriving back in Weymouth from Cherbourg at 00.25 on the Sunday, the *Earl Granville* would sail for Jersey at 13.00, returning directly from there to Portsmouth. The Weymouth-based ferry, *Earl William,* performed a similar schedule in the reverse direction.

During the first weekend of the 'Extended Service', the ferries involved, were the *Earl Granville* and *Earl William*, which in addition to the other two Weymouth-based ships, *Earl Godwin* on the Channel Islands' scheduled duties, and the *Ailsa Princess* on the Cherbourg link, carried over 12,000 passengers and some 2,500 cars between the UK ports of Weymouth and Portsmouth, and the Channel Isles and Cherbourg.

Following privatisation in July 1984, plans were drawn up for a new 'Starliner' service from Portsmouth to the Channel Islands commencing in the spring of 1985, in which the *Earl Granville* was to figure prominently. The 'Starliner' service was to prove expensive from its very inception. The two ships selected for the proposed service from Portsmouth were the *Earl Granville* and *Earl William*, which were sent to a Danish shipyard in Aalborg for major refitting. The total cost for the refit of these two vessels was some £5 million. Completion of the work was delayed at the Danish shipyard due to industrial problems and the luxury service didn't become fully operational until 30th April 1985.

During the following year of 1986, the trading position worsened, despite a strenuous advertising campaign early in the year, including the opening of the *Earl Granville* to the general public at Portsmouth and an introductory visit by the ship to London.

By the end of September, with continued losses at both Portsmouth and Weymouth, Sealink British Ferries decided to close down their services to the

Channel Islands. As a result of the announcement there was strike action in the fleet and the *Earl Granville* did not return to Portsmouth until 18th October. After an idle period, she went for overhaul on 26th February 1987 before picking up a three-week charter for the Ministry of Defence. Under the command of Captain John Attwood, the *Earl Granville* arrived in Marchwood early in March 1987 and proceeded to embark 285 troops, and load their equipment and stores, for an exercise in Norway. She left Marchwood on 12th March and arrived in Bergen for refuelling on the 14th March, departing the following day for Bogen, where she landed the troops and their gear for exercises in Arctic conditions. The Sealink ferry then berthed in the nearby port of Narvik for some ten days. The *Earl Granville* left Narvik on 25th March 1987, and returned to Bogen to embark the British troops for their homeward voyage. Calling at Bergen once again to refuel, she departed from that Norwegian port on 28th March bound for Marchwood, where she arrived shortly before 08.00 on 30th March to land troops and stores following completion of a successful exercise.

Returning to normal service shortly after completion of the MOD Charter, the *Earl Granville* arrived in Weymouth on 10th April and sailed to the Channel Islands two days later, becoming the first ferry to use the new ramp in St. Peter Port. She then returned to Portsmouth, where she opened a new summer link to Cherbourg, the service continuing until the end of September, when the *Earl Granville* was laid up again.

Following an early spring refit in Falmouth, the *Earl Granville* called at Weymouth on 25th March 1988 prior to re-opening the Portsmouth-Cherbourg link on 30th March. She continued on that service for two summers, with a lay up in Weymouth during the intervening winter period, from 27th October until 3rd January 1989. In fact, she left Weymouth for the very last time on 3rd January 1989, bound for Harwich to cover the Hook of Holland service, whilst the *St. Nicholas* went off service for her annual refit. The *Earl Granville* called at Portsmouth en route to Harwich, and later returned to the Hampshire port to

handle the busy Cherbourg programme for the year.

On 19th August 1989 she sustained serious damage, when she hit an underwater obstruction on the approach to Cherbourg Harbour with 700 passengers on board. Consequently the service was suspended for a time, which caused chaos on both sides of the Channel. The freighter *Skarvoy*, was chartered to run in tandem with the *Earl Godwin* at Weymouth to maintain the route. Later, the Isle of Man Steam Packet Company's *Mona's Queen* was chartered and took up the Portsmouth-Cherbourg route on 4th September 1989 but there were difficulties with her as she was only a side-loading vessel and so the *Saint Patrick II* from Irish Ferries took over the route on 15th September.

The *Earl Granville* meanwhile was sent to Le Havre for repairs. Work was not completed until February 1990. She was then sent to the Irish Sea for a month to cover the refits of the *Galloway Princess* and *Darnia*, a job for which she was not entirely suitable.

Following the takeover of Sealink British Ferries by Stena Line in the spring of 1990, the *Earl Granville* was transferred to the Sea Containers' fleet, and saw no further service with Sealink Stena. In fact, she was laid up in the River Fal until the summer, when on 19th July 1990, she returned to the Portsmouth-Cherbourg route on charter to Hoverspeed, in place of the delayed InCat craft the *Hoverspeed Great Britain*. The new fast craft arrived on 14th August 1990 and the *Earl Granville* was then laid up in Southampton and offered for sale.

She was purchased by Agapitos Lines of Greece

A view of the *Earl Granville* pictured at Weymouth in Sealink British Ferries livery in 1988. (*Ambrose Greenway*)

and sailed from Southampton on 12th December 1990 as the *Express Olympia* bound for Piraeus and a new life in the Greek Islands. After only 32 years of service operating under various companies, she went for scrap in 2005, as a victim of Hellas Ferries' obsession with fast ferry operations.

AILSA PRINCESS/EARL HAROLD

The *Ailsa Princess* was built at the Cantieri Navale Breda shipyard in Venice. With a length of 369 feet and a service speed of 20 knots she had a similar outward appearance to her half sister, the *Antrim Princess* also built for the Stranraer-Larne route. She entered service on 7th July 1971 on the North Channel route. In December 1981, it was announced that the *Ailsa Princess* would take over the 1982 summer only service between Weymouth and Cherbourg from the *Maid of Kent,* which had been withdrawn from service the previous autumn. Prior to taking up her new role, however, certain modifications had to be completed to fit the *Ailsa Princess* out for service on the English Channel. A Weymouth crew took over the ship at

Middlesborough on 17th February 1982, and following completion of the refit, the *Ailsa Princess* departed for Weymouth, arriving in the Dorset port on 27th March. With improved facilities for the carriage of freight vehicles, she made a successful trial run to Cherbourg on 31st March, transporting 15 caravans as cargo. This voyage paved the way for the *Ailsa Princess* to open the new season on 2nd April 1982, and she had a most satisfactory summer on the route, proving to be a fitting replacement for the incomparable *Maid of Kent.*

Coincidentally with the introduction of the *Ailsa Princess* on the Weymouth-Cherbourg route, Sealink (UK) Ltd. took over the complete control of the marketing of the service. Previously, the French Railways (SNCF) had had a shared financial interest, and had marketed the operations on the French side of the Channel, but during the spring of 1982, SNCF decided to opt out, leaving Sealink UK to look after the service in its entirety.

At the end of her first summer season on the Weymouth-Cherbourg link, the *Ailsa Princess* left the Dorset port immediately for Folkestone, where she

The **Ailsa Princess** was built for the Stranraer-Larne service. This view shows her coming astern out of Weymouth for Guernsey. *(Miles Cowsill)*

was to relieve the *Horsa* on 2nd October 1982. Following her duties at Folkestone and Holyhead, she was chartered by the Ministry of Defence, and under the command of Captain Martin Scott, himself a RNR Officer, she sailed to Cammell Laird's yard in Birkenhead on 11th November 1982 to prepare for her new venture and to take on stores and equipment. She departed from Birkenhead on 16th November for an exercise laying dummy mines off the Scottish coast, to test the feasibility of using car ferries as mine layers in the event of future hostilities. Completing the charter at the end of November, the *Ailsa Princess* went to Harland & Wolff's yard in Belfast for engine repairs before returning to Weymouth.

The *Ailsa Princess* was in action in the Irish Sea again early in the New Year, when she substituted for the *Manx Viking* on the Heysham-Douglas link prior to opening the summer programme between Weymouth and Cherbourg on 31st March 1983.

For the summer season in 1983, Sealink (UK) Ltd. and the Cunard Line agreed to run more of the short cruises which had proved so popular with the *Maid of Kent* and the *Queen Elizabeth 2* in 1981.

For her third summer season on the Weymouth-Cherbourg route in 1984, the *Ailsa Princess* played her part in commemorating the 40th anniversary of the D Day landings in June, when she transported hundreds of American and Canadian veterans from Weymouth to Cherbourg, enabling them to visit the Normandy beaches once again.

In July 1984, Sealink (UK) Ltd. was privatised, becoming Sealink British Ferries, and plans were formulated almost immediately to change the shape of the Channel Island services from both Weymouth and Portsmouth. Those plans included proposals to inaugurate a 'Starliner' service to the Channel Islands from Portsmouth, employing the *Earl Granville* and the *Earl William*, whilst the *Ailsa Princess* was selected to join the *Earl Godwin* on the newly proposed 'Sunliner' service from Weymouth as from spring of 1985. To prepare for her new work, the *Ailsa Princess* paid her first visit to Jersey for ramp trials on 15th October 1984, creating a record as the largest ferry to berth in St. Helier up to that time. The trip

was also used to pick up a large consignment of trade cars destined for the United Kingdom. The *Ailsa Princess* then sailed on to Guernsey for ramp trials in St. Peter Port, before returning to Weymouth on 16th October 1984, to discharge the trade cars.

Refurbished and repainted in Sealink British Ferries livery at Weymouth during the winter of 1984/85, the *Ailsa Princess* left the Dorset port on 10th January 1985 for Glasgow, where she had a new bow thrust unit fitted to make her more manoeuvrable in port. She then returned to Weymouth for further work locally, prior to taking up her duties on the much publicised 'Sunliner' service from the Dorset port, which was set to commence on 24th May 1985.

In line with the naming policy then in use, the ferry was duly re-Christened on 24th May 1985 as the *Earl Harold* following a competition won by schoolgirl Judith Kempshall. The new Channel Islands' programme had the *Earl Godwin* sailing direct from Guernsey to Weymouth at 07.15, with her sparring partner, the *Earl Harold*, departing Jersey at 07.30, again straight to Weymouth. This meant a quick and direct link with the Dorset port, instead of the old style calls at each island before their eventual departure for Weymouth. Early afternoon sailings from Weymouth at 13.15 to Guernsey, and 15.15 to Jersey, offered a similar service, with both ferries inter-connecting Jersey and Guernsey and then lying alongside overnight. The *Earl Harold* lay alongside in St. Helier and the *Earl Godwin* in St. Peter Port, prior to leaving direct for Weymouth the next morning.

At the end of the summer, in an effort to establish profit-making routes to the Channel Islands once again, a drastic cut was made by Sealink British Ferries at Weymouth with the *Earl Godwin* operating singly on the Channel Islands' service, and the *Earl Harold* earmarked for a return to her old haunts on the Irish Sea. That decision was disastrous for Weymouth, where the 'Sunliner' service had proved to be more popular than the 'Starliner' service at Portsmouth. The main complaint from the daylight voyagers and hoteliers alike, was the sailing programme, which provided for the late arrival of the Weymouth-based ferries in both Jersey and Guernsey.

At the same time, the marketing war which had broken out at Portsmouth between Channel Island Ferries and Sealink British Ferries, appeared to have been won by the former, with their claim to have captured about 80% of the traffic between the Hampshire port and the Channel Islands. Consequently the future of Sealink British Ferries on the Channel Islands' routes began to look bleak.

For 1986, it was announced by Sealink British Ferries that their services to the Channel Islands would run under the 'British Ferries' banner, and that legend was painted on the hulls of the ferries involved, notably those operating in the Western Channel from Weymouth and Portsmouth with British ships and crews. It was also decided that the *Earl Harold* would not be transferred to Irish Sea duties, but would remain on the Channel Isles' working from Weymouth, enabling the *Earl Godwin* to cover the seasonal operations to Cherbourg. But with the latter delayed at refit, and the *Earl William* required in Portsmouth, the Weymouth-Channel Islands service was suspended for a week on 17th February 1986. The *Earl Harold* was drafted in to re-open the route

on 24th February, and remained on the service until the *Earl Godwin* returned to duty on 3rd March. Three weeks later, the *Earl Godwin* opened the summer link with Cherbourg, with the *Earl Harold* working the Channel Isles' service throughout the high season.

As the summer progressed, it became obvious that Channel Island Ferries were gaining ground on Sealink British Ferries on the Portsmouth-Channel Islands link, despite some intensive marketing by the former railway shipping group. The crunch came on 30th September 1986, with the shock announcement that Sealink British Ferries and Channel Island Ferries were to join forces on the Portsmouth-Channel Islands route, and that the proposed merger would result in the formation of British Channel Island Ferries (BCIF), with an all year round programme at Portsmouth. At the same time, it was proposed to maintain a summer only link between the Dorset port and the Channel Islands.

Sealink British Ferries' crews took immediate action, the *Earl Harold,* which had departed Guernsey for Weymouth before the news was

The **Ailsa Princess** loads cars for Cherbourg while the **Earl Godwin** lies over at the port prior to her afternoon sailing. *(Miles Cowsill)*

These two views take in the **Earl Harold** at Weymouth prior to entry into service under her new name on the 'Sunliner' route. *(Ambrose Greenway)*

promulgated, was forced to cruise off the Dorset coast for several hours, in the hope of finding a berth in Weymouth or elsewhere. A berth was found for her in Portsmouth harbour later. The 'Jolly Roger' was flying high as the *Earl Harold* arrived in Portsmouth, and her popular Master, Captain Robin Craythorne, was mildly rebuked by the Queens Harbour Master for authorising the hoisting of such a controversial flag. The *Earl Harold* subsequently returned light to Weymouth, and was laid up indefinitely with the *Earl Godwin*. They were joined by the *Earl William* on the 18th October 1986.

Following all parties agreeing terms, the *Earl Harold* left Weymouth on 4th January 1987 and proceeded to Stranraer, where she relieved on the North Channel route to Larne. Selected for the Weymouth-Cherbourg summer working in 1987, she went to Immingham for dry docking in March, in

An impressive view of the **Earl Harold** at full speed off Guernsey. *(Ambrose Greenway)*

preparation for her seasonal duty, and was back in Weymouth, under the command of genial Captain Mike Leale, to open the link with Cherbourg on 15th April 1987. She kept the service going without major incident until 28th September 1987, when it closed down for the winter period.

In October she was back at Stranraer, covering for the *Galloway Princess* and remained on the North Channel link well into the New Year. The *Earl Godwin*, was laid up on the River Fal until the spring, and when she returned to the Dorset port in May she took up the Cherbourg working again. The *Earl Harold* worked the Weymouth-Cherbourg route for the summer, until the season closed on 3rd October 1988. She ended her days of service from Dorset ports, with the annual Twinning Association charter from Poole to Cherbourg on 5th October, and a Dorset Community Council charter from Weymouth to Cherbourg on 7th October, departing Weymouth a few days later for the very last time. She moved on to Fishguard to relieve the *St. Brendan* on the Rosslare link for four weeks, and followed that duty with a move to Folkestone, where she handled a freight only working to Boulogne.

In January 1989, the *Earl Harold* operated a freight only service between Portsmouth and the Channel Islands, spending her final active days for Sealink British Ferries in the once familiar Channel Isles' trade. She was then chartered by the B&I Line for their Pembroke Dock to Rosslare route in April 1989, registered in Nassau, and painted out in the

company's most attractive blue livery for the summer service. Making her final crossing from Rosslare to Pembroke on 11th October 1989, she sailed shortly afterwards to a lay-up berth in the River Fal, to await disposal.

Early in 1990, the *Earl Harold* was sold to the Samos Shipping Company of Piraeus in Greece, whose operating company was G.A. Ferries, and renamed *Dimitra*. In November 1994, she was then purchased by Agapitos Lines. She spent her last days in Greece operating for Hellas Ferries as the *Express Adonis*. She was sold in 2006 to Mumbai-based Samudera Ferry Shipping & Cruise Services and renamed *New Caribbean Princess*, for a new role on special 12-hour overnight cruises out of Mumbai, India.

EARL WILLIAM

The *Earl William* was purchased in December 1976 by Lloyds Leasing Ltd. of London, on behalf of British Railways for Sealink, for the new ferry service between Portsmouth and the Channel Islands. Built as the *Viking II* by Thoresen Car Ferries, she was launched on 30th April 1964. Having a gross tonnage of 3,670, with her 'sister' the *Viking I*, they were the first drive through car ferries to link United Kingdom ports with those across the Channel. She had space for 180 cars on two vehicle decks and could accommodate 940 passengers.

She was sent to Holyhead, for a major refit. Much of the conversion work was required to be done on the promenade deck, where the couchettes were removed and replaced by upright seating. Where aircraft style seats had existed on the port and starboard sides of the *Viking II*, these were also removed and replaced by more upright seating, the whole area being able to accommodate 258 passengers on completion of the work. The public space amidships was re-designed to include an information bureau, first aid room, tea bar, shops, a storeroom and baggage lockers. Improvements on the boat deck saw more seats installed in the veranda lounge, and the conversion of some crew cabins into ro-ro drivers' accommodation. The cafeteria and saloon forward on that deck were re-designed, to form a cafeteria on the port side of the

The ***Earl Harold*** passes Corbiere lighthouse outward bound for St. Peter Port. *(Ambrose Greenway)*

The *Viking II* was acquired by Sealink in 1976 and following an extensive refit at Holyhead emerged as the *Earl William*. She is seen here leaving St. Helier. *(John Hendy)*

ferry able to seat 86 persons, with a lounge on the starboard side having seating accommodation for 120 weary travellers.

The *Earl William*, quickly established herself on the Portsmouth-Channel Islands circuit, and actually made her first visit to Weymouth for ramp trials on 24th March 1978. Three months later, on 5th June 1978, a second vehicle ramp was opened at the Continental Ferry Port in Portsmouth, and the *Earl*

The *Earl William* at full speed arrives off Jersey inward bound from Weymouth. *(Ambrose Greenway)*

William became the first ro-ro ferry to use the new facility, during what was a relatively successful first year in Sealink colours.

Bad luck struck the *Earl William* on 19th January 1979, however, when one of her propellers became entangled with chains from a buoy off Portsmouth, causing considerable damage to the propeller shaft. She was withdrawn from service for dry docking and repair at Falmouth, leaving the Portsmouth-Channel Islands route without a ship. Without a great deal of thought, British Railways' management decided that it was extremely important to maintain the Portsmouth link with the Channel Isles at the expense of Weymouth, and on 24th January 1979, with the *Caledonian Princess* going off service from Weymouth for her annual refit, it was announced that the Weymouth-Channel Islands route would close temporarily. The *Earl Godwin* was then directed immediately to Portsmouth, to pick up the *Earl William's* programme.

The *Earl William* remained on the Portsmouth-Channel Islands link until March 1981, when she was replaced by the newly acquired *Earl Granville* and then transferred to Weymouth.

On 26th September 1981, the *Earl William* visited Cherbourg for the first time in Sealink colours, when she took a charter party from Weymouth to the French port. It was, in fact, her first voyage to Cherbourg since her days with Townsend Thoresen on the Southampton-Cherbourg working, which had terminated with her sale in 1976. She was, of course, to make many future visits to the French port, especially after the 'Extended Service' had been introduced by Sealink in July 1983.

The *Earl William* ran into difficulties on 5th October 1981, when she was holed off Jersey. She went to Le Havre for dry docking, where approximately 300 square feet of damaged plating was replaced, but her return to service was delayed due to the fact that her main engines and gearbox had to be re-aligned. It was a long and tedious process, and she didn't return to duty until 20th December 1981. The veteran *Maid of Kent* deputised during the early part of her absence, operating the scheduled services and excursions from Weymouth

to Guernsey only, as she was too large to enter the harbour at St. Helier.

Bad luck cast its shadow over the *Earl William* once again in 1982, when on 20th November she struck La Platte Beacon off the Elizabeth Castle breakwater, as she was about to enter St. Helier Harbour after a night crossing from Weymouth. Following a survey, which revealed damage below the waterline, although she wasn't holed, the *Earl William* returned empty to Weymouth, and went on to Falmouth for dry docking and repairs. Her booked passengers were accommodated on the *Earl Granville* and landed in Portsmouth. Meanwhile, the *Earl Godwin's* annual overhaul, which was being dealt with in Weymouth, was rushed through, and she was able to rejoin the Channel Isles' fleet on 26th November 1982.

The *Earl William* finally returned to duty on 18th January 1983, and relieved the *Earl Godwin* at Weymouth, allowing the latter to complete her annual refit locally, although due to bad weather, there were many disruptions to cross-Channel traffic during the

Following the demise of Sealink's operations to the Channel Islands the **Earl William** was chartered by the British Government as a prison ship. She is seen here at Weymouth prior to her departure to Harwich. *(Miles Cowsill)*

early part of the year, and the Channel Islands' services were quite badly hit. Fortunately, bad weather doesn't last forever, though it can be grim in the English Channel at times, and the *Earl William* and the *Earl Godwin* were able to settle down and provide a thoroughly reliable working relationship on the Channel Islands' route from Weymouth during 1983. This was enhanced by the introduction of the 'Extended Service' in July, which saw the *Earl Granville* working out of Weymouth for the first time, as the Weymouth and Portsmouth ferries interchanged at weekends during the high season, bringing calls at Cherbourg into the equation as well as the Channel Islands.

Early in 1984, however, severe weather conditions threatened the whole of the country. As blizzards swept across Scotland and the North of England, Storm Force 10 winds battered the Channel Islands and Channel ports in the south, sending shipping racing for shelter. On 23rd January 1984, the *Earl William*, relieving the *Earl Granville* on the Portsmouth-Channel Islands route, ran into trouble between Guernsey and Jersey, and failed to gain entry to the harbour at St. Helier. Three vehicles were badly damaged as the ferry rolled in heavy seas, when a large unit carrying electrical equipment fell on its side, crushing two privately owned cars. The *Earl William* turned back for Guernsey, but because of the appalling weather, the ship missed out St. Peter Port and headed directly for Portsmouth.

Unfortunately, there were more problems for the *Earl William* ten days later, when she managed to enter St. Peter Port Harbour from Portsmouth on 6th February 1984, but a combination of a bow thrust failure and continuing bad weather in the Channel led to the cancellation of the onward voyage to Jersey. This kept the ferry in harbour overnight, and as a result, the next day's sailing from Portsmouth had to be cancelled too, with passengers and freight being diverted from the Hampshire port to Weymouth for the afternoon departure of the *Earl Godwin*.

On 30th July 1984, Sea Containers Ltd. purchased Sealink (UK) Ltd. for £66 million, with Sealink's fleet of 37 ships operating over 24 routes coming under the umbrella of British Ferries Ltd., a wholly owned subsidiary of Sea Containers Ltd. One of the first plans put forward by the new management team, was for the re-structuring of the Channel Islands' services; the most exciting innovation at that time being the proposal to introduce a luxury night service ('Starliner') from Portsmouth, complemented by a new style day service ('Sunliner') from Weymouth. The *Earl William* would be transferred from Weymouth to Portsmouth to join the *Earl Granville*, and in a blaze of publicity, at a cost of £5 million for the pair, the two ferries were dispatched to a shipyard at Aalborg in Denmark, to be refurbished.

The 'Starliner' service eventually got under way in March 1985, but despite the luxurious appointments on board the two ferries, with evening dinner and a first class breakfast included in the price of the ticket, the huge increase in fares didn't find favour with the travelling public, and, in fact, it heralded an extremely difficult period for Sealink British Ferries on the Channel Islands' routes.

In the following year of 1986, the operations were marketed under the banner of British Ferries, but the result was catastrophic, culminating in the collapse of the services at both Portsmouth and Weymouth. The *Earl William* remained strike bound in Guernsey until 18th October 1986. She then remained at Weymouth until 24th March 1987, when she sailed to a lay-up mooring in the River Fal, pending a firm decision as to her possible use as an immigrant detention ship by the Home Office.

With agreement reached, the *Earl William* was retrieved from her lay-up berth, examined for condition and dispatched to Harwich, where she arrived on 10th May 1987. A special security company was appointed to look after those people who were waiting for their claims to enter Britain to be heard. About half of the 78 potential immigrants held on board the *Earl William* were members of the Tamil minority group in Sri Lanka, who had been involved in hostilities with the Singhalese on the island.

At 05.30 on 16th October 1987, the boredom of those detained on board the *Earl William* was lifted in no uncertain manner when, with the storm spreading eastwards, the ferry broke loose from her moorings at Harwich, and drifted across the River Stour. As she moved away from the quay, she wrecked several yachts and damaged a barge. Both anchors were dropped, but they couldn't hold her in the fierce winds, and even three tugs arriving on the scene couldn't prevent the ferry from grounding off Shotley, on the opposite side of the river to Harwich.

Following the storm, she remained tied up at Parkeston Quay, Harwich, pending a decision as to her future, and on Friday 4th December 1987 she left Harwich for an indefinite lay up in the River Fal. In March 1988, after her enforced winter lay up in the River Fal, the *Earl William* was surveyed and cleaned up in readiness for the opening of a brand new route for Sealink British Ferries between Liverpool and Dun Laoghaire. The *Earl William* inaugurated the service between Liverpool and Dun Laoghaire on 25th April 1988 and despite incurring financial losses, remained on that route until 8th January 1990, when she undertook the final sailing from Merseyside and the service closed down.

Following the demise of the Liverpool-Dun Laoghaire service, the *Earl William* sailed to a lay-up berth in Milford Haven, but she wasn't idle for any length of time, being chartered by Belfast Car Ferries on 29th January 1990 to replace their flagship *St. Colum I*, which had been withdrawn with gearbox trouble. The *Earl William* ran on this working for five weeks until her passenger certificate expired, and she went off to Cardiff for a short refit, with the *St. Colum I* returning to duty on 9th March 1990.

After overhaul, the *Earl William* left South Wales for the Dover Straits, where she relieved the *St. Anselm* on the Folkestone-Boulogne link for two weeks from 6th June. Laid up in the River Fal once again in the autumn of 1990, the *Earl William* was back in action in February 1991, relieving the *Stena Cambria* (undergoing repairs in Falmouth) on the regular Holyhead-Dun Laoghaire working. Following several more short spells of relief work in the spring and early summer of 1991, the *Earl William* was sent to Milford Haven to lay up. She was then required to relieve the *Stena Cambria* once again, and spent a week in the marine yard in Holyhead being cleaned and repainted, finishing with a plain white hull and

The evening sun catches the **Falaise** off Guernsey.
(Ambrose Greenway)

blue funnels before entering service on the Dun Laoghaire route on 29th June 1991. She remained on that link until the *Stena Cambria* returned to duty on 11th July.

After a further period of inactivity, the *Earl William* was put up for disposal, and was purchased by a Greek shipping company in July 1992. She was registered in Malta under her new name *William,* and used on a European Seaways service that provided cut price travel between Italy and Greece. She was renamed *Pearl William* in 1994. In the autumn of 1996, the *Pearl William* was chartered out to another company, P.& L. Ferries, for a service linking Thessaloniki, Istanbul and Odessa. Her name was changed (yet again!) to *Mar Julia,* but, sadly, the enterprise did not live up to expectation, and the service was closed down within a short space of time, with the *Mar Julia* being laid up indefinitely.

Purchased by Stern Lines in February 1998, the car ferry was renamed *Cesme Stern.* Unfortunately, however, her working life was now on a downward slide, and for various reasons, she was placed under arrest in the Italian port of Bari, and remained there in rather a derelict state until she was sold on to a company named Windward Line in the year 2000. Renamed *Windward II,* she was moved across the Adriatic Sea from Bari to a shipyard in the Croatian port of Trogir, where a comprehensive refit was to be

The *Falaise* was converted to a car ferry in 1963 for the Newhaven-Dieppe service and later served on the Channel Islands' operations. *(Ambrose Greenway)*

undertaken, and her hull was returned to the original orange colour always associated with Thoresen Car Ferries. Before the work was completed, however, the money ran out, the refit was aborted, and the vessel detained in Trogir during the period of the dispute.

After lying idle for a long period, the *Windward II* finally left Trogir in the autumn of 2003, bound for the West Indies, where she was earmarked to provide an island cruising service. Her troubles were not over, however, and after colliding with a local naval vessel, she was laid up once again, pending a decision as to her future. Today she is a hotel ship in Trinidad.

FALAISE

The *Falaise* was the first cross-Channel steamer to be built for the Southern Railway after World War II, and when she was delivered to Southampton in June 1947 following her trials, she had accommodation for 1,527 passengers in two classes, and could carry 30 motor cars in the forward hold. She was built by William Denny & Bros. Ltd. of Dumbarton at a cost of £560,000, and launched on 25th October 1946. She was

310 feet long, and had a gross tonnage of 3,710 tons.

The *Falaise* entered service on the Southampton-St. Malo route on 14th July 1947, and five days later, she visited St. Helier for the first time. She continued to operate a direct service between Southampton and Jersey once a week. On 6th September 1947, she made her first visit to St. Peter Port with the mail service from Southampton to the Channel Islands. With mounting losses and after 16 years of loyal service on the Le Havre route the service was closed.

Following weeks of rumours the *Falaise* was finally chosen to open a new ro-ro service between Newhaven and Dieppe as from summer 1964. For her new role extensive work was required to convert her from her role as a classic passenger ship into a stern-loading car ferry. The job took several months, and involved considerable alterations to the passenger accommodation. First and second class were merged, and the *Falaise* became a one-class ship, which was in keeping with British Railways' policy regarding their newly built and converted ferries at the time. A spacious restaurant, with the ship's shop adjacent to

The morning sunshine captures the pretty little **Falaise** outward bound off Noirmont Point. *(Ambrose Greenway)*

it, was situated on B deck aft, with Falaise Bar situated forward on the same deck. A comfortable buffet/lounge was provided on C deck. The cabin accommodation consisted of two-berth cabins, with or without facilities, and a large reclining seat area where motorists could relax. At the same time, her passenger certificate was reduced to 700 passengers. On her car deck she could carry up to 100 vehicles. With completion of the work, the *Falaise* arrived in Newhaven in May 1964 to take up the route and remained there until September 1972.

Following further modification work at Holyhead the *Falaise* was sent to Weymouth. From June to October, her daily programme was a departure from Weymouth at 15.30, arriving in Jersey at 21.30. She remained in St. Helier overnight before leaving for Weymouth at 07.30, with a booked arrival time in the Dorset port of 13.30. She had a most successful first season on the route, with her vehicle deck normally filled to capacity (90 cars) for each voyage, and this resulted in a total of 25,000 cars being conveyed between Weymouth and the Channel Islands during that period.

The **Falaise** prepares to swing in the harbour at Weymouth. *(Ambrose Greenway)*

Sealink (UK) Ltd. responded positively by extending the service to an all year round one, with twice weekly sailings in each direction commencing on 30th October 1973. Guernsey was included in the winter itinerary, with departures for Weymouth at 11.00 on Wednesdays and Fridays, but vehicles had to be craned on and off the ship during this period because St. Peter Port did not become fully operational as a ro/ro port until the summer of 1974.

The *Falaise* was being worked extremely hard in the summer of 1974, however, and becoming subject to frequent minor breakdowns and delays. Something had to give, and it did on 14th August 1974. At the height of the holiday season, and with a packed programme, the *Falaise* had to be taken out of service after she had crawled into Weymouth harbour with yet another late arrival. She was laid up for a time in the Dorset port whilst a thorough inspection was carried out. Fortunately for British Railways, the Swedish car ferry, *Svea Drott*, was temporarily out of work, and she was chartered at short notice to replace the *Falaise,* reporting for duty at Weymouth on 18th August 1974, and picking up the Channel Islands' service on the following day.

Following her checks at Weymouth, the *Falaise* was dispatched to the British Railways' marine yard at Holyhead on 21st August 1974, where her future was to be determined. Unfortunately, so many

mechanical problems surfaced that, because of her age and general condition, she was found to be beyond economical repair. She was put up for disposal, and eventually sold for her scrap value to Spanish ship breakers in Bilbao, leaving Holyhead in tow of the German tug *Fairplay XII* on Christmas Eve 1974, and arriving at her final destination on the last day of the year.

MAID OF KENT

The *Maid of Kent* was launched on 27th November 1958 at William Denny & Bros. at Dumbarton.

With a gross tonnage of 3,920, she was a twin screw steamer and with her two oil-fired steam turbines, she offered a comfortable speed of 20 knots. The *Maid of Kent* was a stern-loading drive on - drive off car ferry, with spaces for 180 motor cars, and was built for the Dover-Boulogne route. She operated on the Dover Strait from 1959 to 1973. The following year she was to open a new joint service between Sealink and SNCF between Weymouth and Cherbourg.

Following a refit of about £100,000 to improve passenger facilities and to modify her stern door to fit the vehicle ramps at Weymouth and Cherbourg. The 'Maid' was considered to be the most suitable ship available for the carriage of coaches and private cars on the newly proposed route to France, although

This view shows the confines of Weymouth harbour with the **Caledonian Princess** and **Maid of Kent**. The Victorian harbour was to be the demise of the port with larger and more economic tonnage coming on stream during the late eighties. *(John Hendy)*

A classic view of the much-loved **Maid of Kent** pictured here at Weymouth following her arrival at the port from Cherbourg. *(John Hendy collection)*

when she arrived in Weymouth following completion of the work in March 1974, she was already 15 years old. Despite her age, however, she was soon to become one of the most popular ferries ever to set sail from the Dorset port.

The new service was to provide daily sailings each way from April to October 1974, with a number of additional night voyages during the peak holiday period. The four-hour crossing was to give convenient day-time passages in both directions, with a 09.45 sailing from Weymouth, and a return departure from Cherbourg at 15.00.

The *Maid of Kent* undertook a trial run on 27th March 1974, which proved to be most successful, and the scene was now set for the inaugural voyage, scheduled for Saturday 6th April, with a morning departure from Weymouth. Unfortunately, the sudden death of French President Pompidou forced the cancellation of the sacred rites usually associated with the opening of a new shipping route.

On the third day of operations, misfortune befell the *Maid of Kent*, when she ran into mechanical difficulties shortly after leaving Weymouth on 9th April 1974. A serious problem had developed in one of her main bearings, and she lay at anchor in Weymouth Bay all day, with 95 outward-bound passengers and their cars remaining on board, as engineers worked desperately to repair the fault. Unfortunately, further examination and new parts were required, and after languishing in Weymouth Bay for eight hours, the *Maid of Kent* limped back into port, assisted by the Admiralty tug, *Sheepdog*. The passengers and cars were offloaded, and arrangements made for some of the travellers to stay in a local hotel at British Railways' expense, whilst others of a more adventurous nature drove off immediately to Southampton, to pick up the night ferry to Le Havre.

Having opened the Cherbourg link from Weymouth just three days prior to that breakdown, the normally reliable *Maid of Kent* was to remain out of service for three weeks, whilst urgent engine repairs were carried out. Fortunately, the *Normannia,* was available, and she was hastily summoned from the Straits of Dover to pick up the Weymouth-Cherbourg timetable, and she remained on the Weymouth payroll for three weeks, making her final crossing on 29th April 1974, which coincided conveniently with the return to duty of the *Maid of Kent.*

As far as the *Maid of Kent* was concerned, a breakdown of that nature was quite rare but following her return to service, she ran into more trouble on 28th May 1974, when she struck a ramp in Cherbourg Harbour, buckling her plating. She arrived back in Weymouth 27 hours late (on 29th May), and Cozens & Company, the local marine engineers, carried out repairs throughout the night. This allowed the *Maid of Kent* to sail on schedule at 09.45 on 30th May 1974.

It is pleasing to record that after the second major incident in less than two months, Weymouth's 'Pocket Liner' continued to work the Cherbourg route without mishap for the rest of the season, providing a safe, comfortable and friendly service for all travellers wishing to cross the Western Channel to France from Weymouth.

Laid up for the winter period at Weymouth in October 1974, the *Maid of Kent* was brought out of hibernation in late March 1975 and dispatched to Stranraer, where she covered for the *Ailsa Princess* on

the North Channel route to Larne for a month, whilst the latter was undergoing a refit. The ship returned to Weymouth on 26th April 1975 to take up the summer service to Cherbourg, operating right through to the end of September.

Day and night crossings were offered in the 1976 season and the route closed again on 16th October 1976 for the winter period.

Prior to the commencement of the 1977 Weymouth to Cherbourg summer programme, the *Maid of Kent* made a one off sailing to Guernsey, with a backlog of trade cars that had built up on the quay at Weymouth. With the busy Easter holiday period fast approaching, the regular Channel Islands' ferries were fully occupied, and it was left to the Cherbourg ferry to transport 196 motor vehicles to St. Peter Port on 6th April 1977. Most of those trade cars were destined for Jersey, but had to be landed in St. Peter Port, as the *Maid of Kent* was too large to enter harbour at St. Helier at that time.

The 1977 summer season passed without incident, but when the *Maid of Kent* went for her annual overhaul in the spring of 1978, her keel was found to have corrosion problems, which required rectification before she was able to commence her duties on the Weymouth-Cherbourg route. Her return to Weymouth was delayed, and the Dover ferry *Lord Warden*, opened the link to the Cherbourg service on 20th March 1978, and she remained on the route for three weeks until the *Maid of Kent* made her appearance on 9th April.

On 1st August 1978, the 100th anniversary of the Weymouth-Cherbourg service was celebrated, albeit in a small way. Originally opened by the Great Western Railway Company in 1878, the route was worked in those early days by the paddle steamers *Great Western* and *South of Ireland*, the latter making the first voyage from Cherbourg to Weymouth, where she arrived an hour late. The normal time for the crossing all those years ago was six hours. In celebration of the centenary of the very first voyage, Sealink organised a programme of activities on board the *Maid of Kent* on that August day in 1978.

The *Maid of Kent* had an excellent summer in 1978, carrying 182,000 passengers and 41,600 motor cars to and from their holiday destinations, an increase of 30% on the previous year. Her seasonal job on the Weymouth-Cherbourg route terminated on 14th October.

The *Maid of Kent* was due to winter over in Weymouth Harbour when the 1979 summer programme came to an end, but on 29th October 1979, she was dispatched to Holyhead to replace the *St. Columba,* which had been withdrawn from service with mechanical problems. After spending part of the winter period in Weymouth, the *Maid of Kent* was dispatched to Smith's Yard in Middlesborough in February 1980 for her annual refit. This ensured her readiness to re-open the seasonal Cherbourg link from Weymouth, which she did with a departure from the Dorset port on Wednesday 2nd April 1980. When the 1980 season opened, it was not generally known that it would be the penultimate one for the *Maid of Kent* on the Cherbourg route.

It was a good summer for the *Maid of Kent*, and it passed without a major incident except for industrial action by French fishermen in the August. The dispute came to a head on 16th August, when 15

French ports were blockaded by fishing boats. The *Maid of Kent* had departed from Weymouth with 500 passengers and 100 motor cars on board, but she was unable to dock in Cherbourg, and remained at anchor for much of the day before returning to Weymouth. The frustrated passengers were given refreshments on return, and allowed to remain on board overnight. The Weymouth-Cherbourg service was suspended, and many passengers took their vehicles or went by coach to Dover to board ferries to Ostend. At the time, a backlog of cars was starting to build up in Cherbourg and other French ports, and there were reports of 25-mile traffic queues in some areas. A truce was called on 19th August, and the *Maid of Kent* managed to get into Cherbourg twice. She brought out over 1,000 passengers and 239 cars on her two visits. Then the French fishermen's attitude hardened, and the blockade was reinforced.

Four days later, on 23rd August 1980, the *Maid of Kent,* lying idle in Weymouth Harbour, was opened to the general public, and remained open for six days (09.30 to 16.30), during which time nearly 15,000 visitors had poured up the gangway at 25p a time. At

The **Maid of Kent** leaves Weymouth on her last sailing to Cherbourg prior to being withdrawn from service. *(Brian Searle collection)*

long last, however, on 29th August 1980, the blockade was lifted, and the *Maid of Kent* took off on a night run to Cherbourg with 81 passengers and 18 cars. She returned to Weymouth at 08.00 the next day with 360 passengers, 85 motor cars and 25 caravans. The rest of the summer passed without further trouble with the last scheduled voyage being made on Friday 3rd October.

The final voyage of the season took place on Saturday 4th October 1980, with a Conservative Euro excursion to Cherbourg, the first political rally to be held outside territorial waters.

The *Maid of Kent's* last day of operations on the Weymouth-Cherbourg route dawned on 2nd October 1981. Dressed overall, she got a noisy send off from enthusiasts gathered on the quay, and from crew members of the *Earl William* moored ahead of her. With her whistle screaming almost continuously, she left Weymouth Harbour on her final run to Cherbourg. Many regulars paid their respects on that unique occasion, chief of whom was retired RAF Squadron Leader Peter Hands, who was notching up a total of 105 day trips on the *Maid of Kent* in five years, and they all referred to the special place the splendid car ferry had secured in the port of Weymouth's maritime history.

After a faultless voyage, all flags were flying high as with impeccable time keeping, Senior Master, Captain Michael Hurd-Wood, eased her into her berth alongside the quay, right opposite the Gare Maritime in Cherbourg. Local representatives of Sealink and of the Cherbourg port authority came on board, and Derek Shorter, Sealink's area manager in Southampton, presented a memento in the form of a *Maid of Kent* life belt, to the Chairman of the local Chamber of Commerce.

The *Maid of Kent* left the French port promptly at 15.00 (local time), and with 'La Marseillaise' ringing out over the public address system she set out on her final crossing to Weymouth.

The *Earl William,* operating on the Channel Isles' route, fouled an underwater obstruction near St. Helier on 5th October 1981, and had to retire to Le Havre for dry docking and repairs. The *Maid of Kent* was immediately pressed into service to cover the working from Weymouth, but she was only able to

The **Maid of Kent** laid up at Newhaven prior to her disposal to Spanish ship-breakers. *(Miles Cowsill)*

visit Guernsey, as she was too large to berth in St. Helier at that time. The *Maid of Kent* kept the link between Weymouth and St. Peter Port open until 30th October 1981, when she made Sealink's very last steam-powered crossing.

On her arrival in Weymouth she was de-stored, and she remained in the Dorset port for some three weeks, before being dispatched to a lay-up berth in Newhaven on 24th November. Put up for disposal, she was sold to Spanish breakers in Pasajes, leaving under tow for the Spanish port at 23.00 on 10th April 1982.

NORMANNIA

When, in 1950, the British Transport Commission ordered a new cross-Channel ferry to replace the ageing *Hantonia* on the Southampton-Le Havre service, she was also intended as running mate for the former Southern Railway passenger steamer, *Falaise,* which was employed on the Southampton-St. Malo route.

The *Normannia* was 309 feet long, with a breadth of 49 feet and a gross tonnage of 3,543. She had a certificate for 1,410 passengers in two classes (780 in first class and 630 in third), and she could carry up to 12 motor cars, which had to be craned on board. Built by William Denny Bros. Ltd., of Dumbarton in Scotland, the *Normannia* was the last railway passenger steamer to be built for the cross-Channel services operating from Southampton and was launched on 19th July 1951. She was delivered to Southampton six months later, where she was registered, and sailed on her maiden voyage on the all year round service to Le Havre on 3rd March 1952.

As built, her passenger accommodation comprised a number of two-berth de luxe cabins, together with one, two and three-berth cabins in first class, with some additional berths in the first class ladies' room. Her very satisfactory third class facilities included one and two-berth cabins, with extra berths being provided in separate sections for ladies and gentlemen. The term 'third class' was abolished shortly after the *Normannia* entered service, and from then until 1964, two-class ships carried first and second class status. From March 1964, all British Railways' ferries were designated one-class ships.

The *Normannia* made her first visit to the Channel Islands on a relief duty from Southampton on 13th November 1958 and a little over a year later, she appeared in Weymouth for the first time, when she took over the Channel Isles' service from the *St. Patrick,* on 2nd January 1960. This was at the time when the locally celebrated former Great Western Railway pair, *St. Julien* and *St. Helier* were laid up for the whole of the winter period of 1959/1960. The *Normannia* returned to Southampton on 24th February 1960, but was seen in Weymouth on a Channel Isles' working again in 1963 when she replaced the *Caesarea* from 12th to 20th March, whilst the latter was off station being fitted with a new compass.

Returning to her regular spot on the Southampton-Le Havre route, the *Normannia* made her final sailing from the French port on 3rd December 1963, de-stored, and then proceeded to Hawthorn, Leslie's yard on the Tyne, for conversion to a stern-loading car ferry for the Dover-Boulogne link. The work took some four months at a cost of over £250,000. She entered service on the Boulogne service on 21st April 1964. She could now, carry 110 motor cars on her two vehicle decks, 68 being stowed on the main car deck with 42 on the upper deck, access to which was by means of a folding ramp but her passenger accommodation was reduced to 500.

Extensive changes were made to the passenger accommodation, particularly on the main and upper decks, where spaces for vehicles had been acquired at the expense of cabins and public rooms. The bridge deck was extended to the stern, and the old lower saloon converted for the stowage of vehicles. To offset those losses, a self-service cafeteria, buffet, ticket office, bureau de change and a passport office were installed on the promenade deck, and on completion of all that reconstruction work, the gross tonnage of the *Normannia* was reduced from 3,543 to 2,217.

The newly converted car ferry was to remain on the Straits of Dover for quite some time, although she was called upon to relieve the *Falaise,* also recently converted to carry cars, on the Newhaven-Dieppe run late in 1964, and again in 1965. There was a

The **Normannia** at the lay-up berth at Weymouth. *(Ferry Publications Library)*

change in routine yet again in the summer of 1965, when, following the delay in completion of Sealink's Irish Sea ferry, *Holyhead Ferry I,* the *Normannia* was selected to inaugurate the car ferry service between Holyhead and Dun Laoghaire on 9th July for ten days until the new ferry arrived.

The *Normannia* then returned to the Straits of Dover for a lengthy spell, which included a short period of relief work to inaugurate the Harwich-Hook of Holland route in October 1968. In the spring of 1973, she was transferred to the French Railways (SNCF), to replace the passenger steamer *Cote d'Azur*, being newly registered in Calais, and flying the French flag for the whole of the summer season.

Returning to British Railways' control in the autumn, she was re-registered in London and then sent to Weymouth on 18th December 1973, to relieve the crippled *Falaise* on the Channel Islands' working. Completing that duty on 15th March 1974 she returned to Dover, but was back in Weymouth in less than four weeks to take over the brand new Cherbourg service, after the *Maid of Kent* developed engine trouble just three days into the new working

on 9th April 1974. The *Normannia* made her final crossing from Cherbourg on 29th April 1974 but was retained at Weymouth, replacing the unfortunate *Falaise* once again on the Channel Islands' link until 20th May.

Returning to work in the Straits of Dover, the *Normannia* ran into trouble herself on 9th July 1974 when she hit the remains of the old paddle steamer berth off the Admiralty Pier in Dover Harbour. With the engine room and main car deck flooded, she was in grave danger of sinking in the harbour. She was rescued by tugs and taken to the tidal basin, where she was patched up temporarily before being towed to Middlesborough for major repairs, an expensive job which lasted for almost three months.

Now beginning to show evidence of age, the *Normannia* continued on the Weymouth-Channel Islands ro-ro service single-handed throughout the winter and spring of 1974/75. Indeed, she maintained the link right up until 15th July 1975, completing 170 consecutive round trips, thus making what was believed to have been the longest unbroken spell of duty ever recorded by a Sealink vessel on that route.

The **Normannia** was built as an overnight passenger ship for the Southampton - Le Havre route and converted to a Dover - Boulogne car ferry in 1964. In April 1978 she operated on the Channel Islands' service in partnership with the **Viking Victory** from Townsend Thoresen. *(Kevin Le Scelleur)*

She then went back to the Straits of Dover and later to a lay-up berth in Newhaven Harbour, for much of the winter period of 1975/76. She was rushed into service at Weymouth once again at the end of March, to handle the backlog of passengers and cars which had built up as a result of the withdrawal of the *Earl Godwin* from service with serious generator trouble on 23rd March 1976.

The *Normannia* left Weymouth on 26th March 1976 with a full load of motor cars (110), but the 1,000 passengers who had also booked on the *Earl Godwin*, were taken to the Channel Islands on board the comfortable and ever faithful *Sarnia*. The *Earl Godwin* returned to service on 6th April, with the veteran *Normannia* remaining as standby vessel for a few days in case of further trouble. The *Normannia* was then laid up in Newhaven at the end of the 1976 summer season. After a relatively peaceful summer, in which she completed her final season between July and September 1977, on the Dover-Boulogne link, the *Normannia* was again laid up in Newhaven and put up for disposal. Before a sale could be arranged, however, she was summoned out of 'retirement' in January 1978, to replace the *Horsa* at Folkestone, after the latter was storm damaged and required dry docking in Calais.

With the *Horsa* back in action in March 1978, the *Normannia* was then despatched to Weymouth to deputise for the *Earl Godwin* on the Channel Isles' route, whilst the latter was strike bound at refit. The *Normannia* ran from Weymouth in partnership with the *Caledonian Princess* for the last ten days in March, until she was relieved by the chartered Townsend Thoresen ferry, *Viking Victory.* The *Normannia* then went for lay up, but with Weymouth's *Earl Godwin* still delayed at the shipyard, and the *Caledonian Princess* also off service for her own annual inspection, she was recalled again to the Dorset port on 11th April 1978, to partner the *Viking Victory* on the Weymouth-Channel Isles route.

As the month of April progressed, however, life on board the *Normannia* was becoming almost intolerable, particularly in the stewards' quarters, due to an internal oil leak. In fact, members of the catering staff night stopping with the ship in St.

Helier, were found accommodation ashore in guesthouses, so bad did the problem become. Oil to the depth of several inches lapped around the alleyways and into cabins, requiring visitors to certain parts of the ship to don protective clothing. Some of the passengers' accommodation was affected, too, and the embarkation of all passengers was eventually abandoned. In the end the *Caesarea* had to be brought in from Dover. She arrived from the Kentish port to run in tandem with the *Normannia,* carrying passengers, whilst their cars were conveyed on board the stricken car ferry. These circumstances prevailed for some three weeks, until both vessels made their final voyages from the Channel Islands to Weymouth on 6th May 1978.

The *Normannia,* in a somewhat unserviceable state, returned to her lay-up berth in Newhaven, and was again put up for disposal. In October 1978, a sale was arranged with Red Sea Ferries of Dubai but final agreement was not forthcoming even though her place of registry had been changed to Panama. She was eventually purchased by Spanish ship breakers, Desguaces Heme S.A. of Gijon and on 29th November left Newhaven at 16.25, bound initially for Falmouth for bunkers. She arrived there at 08.30 on the following day and took on sufficient fuel and fresh water for the voyage to Gijon but foul weather delayed the vessel's departure until 2nd December. She finally left at 20.25 bound for Brest in France but serious trouble developed off the Cornish coast when the ship's fuel became contaminated with water and a boiler was extinguished. Captain Jarvis had to drop anchor to avoid a collision with a Russian factory ship and to allow Chief Engineer Brian Saunders and his team time to separate the water from the oil in order to raise precious steam again. The *Normannia* eventually reached Brest at 08.50 on 3rd December, and after spending the morning at anchor, berthed at 14.40. Much needed fresh water was taken on board but unfortunately there wasn't any oil fuel available locally. Following urgent telecommunications with Sealink H.Q., two road tankers arrived in Brest at 20.00 on 4th December, providing oil for the ship. With bunkering complete, the *Normannia* left Brest just after midnight on 5th December, and arrived in

Gijon after an uneventful voyage across the Bay of Biscay, entering the Spanish port at 01.00 on 6th December and tying up at her last resting place at the breaker's yard at 08.45.

PORTELET

The *Portelet* arrived at Weymouth in spring 1987, following the closure of Sealink British Ferries' services to the Channel Islands in September 1986. The *Portelet* had been built at Cammell Laird's shipyard on Merseyside in 1966/67, for the Burns and Laird Lines' service between Ardrossan and Belfast. She was built with a certificate for 1,200 passengers, and could carry 140 cars.

She made her maiden voyage from the Scottish terminal on 3rd January 1968. Her pattern of sailings allowed for a departure from Ardrossan at 10.00 and Belfast at 16.30, she provided daily crossings in each direction, with a duration of voyage of $4\frac{1}{2}$ hours.

The Burns and Laird Company was a subsidiary of the Coast Lines Group, and when the organisation was bought out by P&O in 1971, the *Lion* fell into the hands of the new owners and with the 'troubles' seriously affecting traffic on the Ulster link in 1976, she was transferred to a new service between Dover and Boulogne. The *Lion* remained on the Dover-Boulogne working until 1985, when, in January of that

year, the P&O routes from Dover to Boulogne and from Southampton to Le Havre, were purchased by Townsend Thoresen. The ship was not required by her new owners and was sold to Marlines of Limassol, Cyprus. She was renamed *Baroness M* and underwent major conversion work to operate as a night ferry on a weekly service between Patras (Greece), Ancona in Italy and Ismir in Turkey.

The alterations to the ship included the replacement of the forward lounge on the boat deck and the cafeteria on the main deck by four-berth cabins enhanced by private facilities and the provision of couchettes below the car deck. A new lounge was constructed on the boat deck level. This was fully carpeted and a large coffee shop, duty free shop and boutique also installed. The new arrangements provided sleeping accommodation for 384 persons in four-berth cabins with a further 118 places in the couchettes. There were also Pullman style seats available for an additional 188 weary travellers.

Despite all that refurbishment work, however, the *Baroness M* was not required for the route and was put on the charter market. With nothing else available, she was promptly chartered by British Channel Island Ferries for their newly proposed summer only service between Weymouth and the

The **Portelet** (formerly the **Lion**) was built for the Ardrossan-Belfast service. *(Miles Cowsill)*

Channel Islands, as from April 1987. She arrived in Weymouth, under her new name, *Portelet,* on 5th April 1987. She then proceeded almost immediately to Portsmouth, to cover for the British Channel Island Ferries' flagship, *Corbiere,* on the Channel Islands' service from the Hampshire port, but unfortunately, due to major problems associated with some of the cabins which had been constructed in Greece, not least of which was the inability of the sprinkler system to function in those cabins, the Department of Trade refused to grant a full passenger certificate, and about one third of the cabins were temporarily closed down.

The *Portelet* returned to Weymouth in time to open the Channel Islands' service on 15th April 1987. As a result of the Department of Trade's refusal to grant a full passenger certificate, British Channel Island Ferries (BCIF) were forced to run Truckline's ferry, *Cornouailles,* in tandem with her, to meet demand. In fact, 120 passengers and 17 cars had to be offloaded before the vessel sailed on the inaugural voyage from Weymouth, those being transferred to the *Cornouailles.* A total of 480 passengers and 93 motor cars finally set sail on the *Portelet*, which arrived late in Jersey. Ironically, her support ship, the *Cornouailles,* arrived on time! The latter remained on the Weymouth-Channel Isles route for several days, whilst work was carried out

almost continuously on board the *Portelet,* in order to meet the requirements of the Department of Trade as quickly as possible.

Despite the rather complicated start, the *Portelet* had a fairly successful first season on the route and by late September 1987, she had carried nearly 138,000 passengers and some 28,000 motor cars between Weymouth and the Channel Islands. Her final voyage from the Dorset port to the Channel Islands departed at 22.45 on Friday 25th September, arriving in Guernsey at 06.45 and Jersey at 09.15 on Saturday 26th September 1987. On the following Sunday, the *Portelet* made a special trip to Portsmouth with National Craft Fair exhibitors on board. Leaving St. Helier at 20.00, she called at St. Peter Port to embark more passengers, and arrived in Portsmouth at 07.00 on Monday 28th September 1987. She later returned to Weymouth to de-store and lay up whilst awaiting further instructions. Not required by her owners, or for additional charter work during the winter period of 1987/88, she remained berthed alongside the Cargo Stage in Weymouth Harbour, although the name *Portelet* was removed and replaced by *Baroness M.*

In the spring of 1988, the vessel was again chartered by British Channel Island Ferries for another summer season on the Weymouth-Channel Islands link, and the name *Portelet* was repainted on the hull. There had been some complaints about the lack of comfortable

The **Portelet** arrives at St. Peter Port on a delayed morning sailing from Jersey. *(Miles Cowsill)*

Sealink chartered the **Prins Philippe** to maintain the Weymouth-Cherbourg route in 1985. *(Joe Ward)*

seating for the increased number of passengers carried during the first charter the previous year, and BCIF now moved to improve the quality of the passenger accommodation and other facilities, by spending over £200,000 on the provision of 300 extra Pullman style seats in the upper lounge and elsewhere around the ship, completely carpeting the public rooms, and generally creating a cosy atmosphere on board, with a friendly crew, some of whom had served on board the *Lion* in her days with P&O.

The new season was due to open on Wednesday 6th April 1988, and close on 1st October. The new ship's timetable showed a dramatic change from the previous year, with a daily departure from Weymouth at 13.30. Arrivals in St. Peter Port and St. Helier were at 17.30 and 20.30 respectively, with night sailings from the Channel Islands enabling the ferry to arrive in Weymouth at 06.45. The *Portelet* had a moderately successful second season on the Channel Islands' route, although it was noticeable that Condor Ferries' fast services to the Islands were beginning to bite into the passenger figures. So when the *Portelet* made her final crossing on 1st October 1988, she brought to an end British Channel Island Ferries' interest in Weymouth.

Back in Greece, the *Baroness M* entered service between Larnaca in Cyprus, and Jounieh in the Lebanon. In Piraeus during the winter of 1996/97, the *Baroness M* was sold to Equester Shipping, and on 24th January 1997 she left the Mediterranean Sea forever, when she sailed for Indonesia and a new life in the former Dutch East Indies.

The *Baroness M* remained in action in that area for a considerable period of time before being withdrawn from service during winter 2003/4, put up for disposal, and sold for scrap to ship breakers in Bangladesh in March 2004. She arrived at her final destination, Chittagong Roads, in Bangladesh on 12th April 2004.

PRINS PHILIPPE

When the Belgian vessel, *Prins Philippe,* arrived in Weymouth in the spring of 1985 to cover the seasonal service to Cherbourg, she became, at over 5,000 gross tons, the largest ferry ever to enter harbour at the Dorset port. Built as a replacement for the veteran passenger vessel *Koning Albert*, on the Straits of Dover, with two trips daily from Ostend, the *Prins Philippe* was the first Belgian drive through car ferry but proved inflexible as she was fitted with a fixed mezzanine deck with a capacity for 230 cars. Passenger capacity was for 1,240.

By 1985, the *Prins Philippe* had operated in the Straits of Dover for nearly 12 years, and was the

The **Prins Philippe** arrives at Cherbourg on her morning sailing from Dorset. *(Miles Cowsill)*

spare ship in the RTM fleet. She was chartered at very short notice in the spring of that year by Sealink British Ferries for their Weymouth-Cherbourg route, after the latter company had failed to secure the anticipated services of the Isle of Man Steam Packet Company's ferry, *Manx Viking,* for the summer season. In any case, the passenger-carrying capacity of the *Manx Viking,* would not have been sufficient for the heavy weekend bookings expected on the Weymouth-Cherbourg link during the 1985 summer period. In the event, the *Prins Philippe* wasn't available to open the service on 1st April, and the car ferry *Thjelvar* was hastily chartered from her Swedish owners as an early substitute.

The *Prins Philippe* finally took up station at Weymouth on 6th May 1985, and proved to be more than an adequate replacement for the *Ailsa Princess,* which had operated the Weymouth-Cherbourg route during the three previous summers. It was with some regret that the Cherbourg programme for 1985 was restricted to a single daily round trip, without the overnight crossings in July and August, which had been a feature in previous years.

Nevertheless, the *Prins Philippe* had a most successful summer employed on the Weymouth-Cherbourg link, the undoubted highlight being the

record-breaking run on 20th August 1985, when she knocked 20 minutes off the existing record set up in 1910 by the Great Western Railway Company's steamer *Ibex,* thus claiming the Blue Riband of the Western Channel.

The *Prins Philippe* made her final return crossing between Weymouth and Cherbourg on 29th September 1985, and following her charter work for Sealink British Ferries, she was returned to her owners and put up for disposal. She was later purchased by Moby Lines of Italy, for their service between La Spezia, Livorno and Bastia (the principal city in Sardinia). In November 1993, the *Moby Love* was sold on to the Greek company, Ventouris Sea Lines, partly rebuilt and renamed *Panagia Tinou 2.* However, within two years, with loans and interest outstanding, she was seized by the National Bank of Greece and laid up in Piraeus. In October 1998, the *Panagia Tinou 2* was purchased by Agapitos Express and renamed *Express Athina*, but within a year, she had been sold yet again, this time to Hellenic Seaways of Piraeus. Today she operates for SAOS Ferries in the Adriatic Sea under her new name *Express Limnos.* The vessel spent most of 2009 laid up at Lavrion south of Athens, with owners having no use for her in the current economic climate.

5. Brief Visitors to Weymouth

CORNOUAILLES/HAVELET

The *Cornouailles* made her first appearance at Weymouth on 15th April 1987, running the first few days of the new summer service to the Channel Islands in place of the *Portelet*. In 1989, the *Cornouailles* was transferred to BCIF, painted out in that company's livery, renamed *Havelet* and assigned to the Poole - Channel Islands route to work with the larger *Rozel*. The *Havelet* was acquired by Condor Ferries to operate on the Weymouth-Channel Islands route, following the demise of BCIF, as foul weather support ship for that company's fast craft operations. Following the Maritime & Coastguard Agency inspection of the ship, many defects were found with her and the end of the year was set as a deadline for completion of these works. As a result, the *Havelet* was withdrawn from service by Condor and she made her final crossing from the Channel Islands on 28th October 1996, after which she was laid up in Portland Harbour for quite some time until her safety problems had been resolved. The required work was completed, she was brought back into service as a standby vessel in November 1998, and she continued in that role until October 1999, when she was laid up in Weymouth Harbour and employed as an accommodation ship pending disposal.

She was later sold to Montenegro Lines in 2000. She was renamed *Sveti Stefan* and sailed from Weymouth for the very last time on 25th August 2000, bound for Bar and a new career in the Adriatic Sea.

EARL SIWARD

After a long period of service with Sealink on the English Channel and Irish Sea, the *Earl Siward* was sent to Weymouth at the end of her career to substitute for the crippled *Earl William* on the Weymouth-Channel

Truckline's **Cornouilles,** later renamed **Havelet**, arrives at Weymouth in April 1987. *(Brian Searle collection)*

The **Earl Siward** arrives at Weymouth whilst on the Channel Islands' service in 1981. *(Collection of the late Arthur Russell)*

Isles service. The *Earl William* had been holed in two places when she struck a rock at the entrance to St. Helier Harbour, and was rushed to Falmouth for urgent repairs. In her absence, the *Earl Siward* made three round voyages from Weymouth to the Channel Islands on 11th/12th/13th July 1981. With an overall length of 369 feet, she was the longest ship ever to enter St. Helier up to that time. This was her last operation with Sealink, she was then sent to Newhaven and placed on the disposal list. She was purchased by Sol Ferries Ltd. of Cyprus and left Newhaven on 25th November 1981. Her new owners, who received 70% funding from the Government of Cyprus, planned to operate the vessel on a passenger/freight service between Greece and Italy. Renamed *Sol Express*, she had an extensive refit in Perama prior to entering service from Patras to Brindisi. Public rooms were upgraded, and sleeping berths for passengers were increased to 300 to prepare her for her new role.

The *Sol Express* remained in service with the Cypriot company for some four years, when she was deemed to be surplus to requirements, and laid up in Limassol. Put up for disposal, she was purchased by

the Quadrini Group, a British consortium based in the north-east of England. She left Limassol under tow in mid-March 1986, finally arriving in Newcastle on 18th April 1986. Renamed the *Tuxedo Royale*, the old Sealink car ferry was refitted at great expense to replace the *Tuxedo Princess* (the former *Caledonian Princess*) as a floating entertainment centre under the bridge at Gateshead on the Tyne, and in July 1988, the latter was taken under tow to the Clyde, where she berthed at Anderston Quay. The *Tuxedo Royale* remained as a floating nightclub at Gateshead for nearly ten years. In March 2000, the *Tuxedo Royale* was towed to Middlesborough, where she was re-registered and once again refitted and repainted, in order to perform a similar role on Teeside.

After some four years of poor trading as a floating entertainment centre near the Riverside Stadium in Middlesborough, the operation was closed down in March 2004.

ISLE OF GUERNSEY

The *Isle of Guernsey* made her first visit to Weymouth in July 1953, but it was to be another eight years before she entered the Dorset port again, and this was at Easter time in 1961, after all passenger traffic to the Channel Islands had been transferred to Weymouth. She was required urgently to take a considerable number of airline passengers, who had been left behind at Weymouth by a fully loaded *Caesarea* and were housed in the Pavilion Theatre overnight. The *Isle of Guernsey,* having arrived in Jersey from Southampton, sailed 'light' to Weymouth early on Good Friday morning, to pick up the passengers who had been left behind on the previous evening.

The *Isle of Guernsey* returned to Weymouth on 13th May 1961, which was the opening day of the new service from the Dorset port to the Channel Islands, and she remained on the route for four weeks as cover for the brand new passenger ferry *Sarnia,* due from her builders on the Isle of Wight but slightly delayed. The *Isle of Guernsey* made her final voyage from the Channel Islands to Weymouth on 10th June 1961, which coincided with the arrival of the *Sarnia,* and left almost immediately for Southampton to lay up pending disposal.

LA DUCHESSE DE BRETAGNE

La Duchesse de Bretagne was the former British Railways' *Brighton,* built for the Newhaven-Dieppe service during the post-war era. Following her disposal by British Railways, she was purchased by Jersey Lines in December 1966, a small Channel Island based company that had previously bought the former GWR tender *Sir Richard Grenville* for service between Jersey and Granville. Plans for the *Brighton* included a series of scheduled sailings and excursions linking Weymouth and Torquay with the Channel Islands, St. Malo and Cherbourg. The vessel was renamed *La Duchesse de Bretagne* prior to being sent to a shipyard in Antwerp in January 1967 for a major

The *Isle of Guernsey* swings in Weymouth harbour inward bound from the Channel Islands. Further up the harbour is the cargo ship the *Roebuck*. *(The Late John Chambers collection)*

refit, during which she was fitted with ramps on both sides near the stern. This enabled about 20 cars to be driven on board and stowed on the open deck.

The original proposals for Jersey Lines' summer schedule included a car ferry service between Weymouth and the Channel Islands and Cherbourg, but these plans were dropped in July 1967, because the private company was only permitted to ship cars not taken by British Railways' cargo ships, which were few in number, and made it a very uneconomical proposition. Four car-carrying day cruises from Weymouth to Cherbourg were also cancelled, and replaced by day cruises from Torquay.

Jersey Lines continued the twice weekly day cruises for foot passengers from Weymouth to Jersey and Guernsey, and despite the early season car-carrying frustrations at Weymouth, by the time the summer season had ended on 27th September 1967, *La Duchesse de Bretagne* had carried over 80,000 passengers and some 1,500 motor cars to and from the UK ports of Weymouth and Torquay. Regrettably, Weymouth was not included in the sailing schedules for 1968, and, in fact, this was to be the final year for

the company, which went into administration in 1969. *La Duchesse de Bretagne* was arrested by the Admiralty Marshall, and she lay in Portsmouth Harbour for quite some time as attempts were made to resolve her owners' financial problems. Sadly, no offer of salvation was forthcoming, and she was finally sold for scrap and towed ignominiously to a breaker's yard in Bruges, Belgium, where she arrived on 14th February 1970.

LISIEUX

The *Lisieux* appeared in Weymouth during the summer of 1965, after a relatively short career of only 12 years operating between Dieppe and Newhaven. With British Railways acting as agents for the French Line, Weymouth featured prominently in the ferry's itinerary on Thursdays and Fridays for seven weeks from 12th August to 2nd October 1965. The *Lisieux* would arrive in the Dorset port from St. Malo on the Thursday evening, embark passengers early on Friday morning for a day trip to Guernsey, returning to Weymouth from St. Peter Port during Friday evening to land the day-trippers, and then take on

The **La Duchesse de Bretagne** (ex **Brighton**) at Weymouth during her short-lived English Channel operation with Jersey Lines. *(John Hendy collection)*

The **Lisieux** at Weymouth in 1965 operating under French Line. *(Colin Caddy)*

passengers for a night crossing to St. Malo. At the close of this most interesting and varied programme of excursions, which, incidentally, was not overwhelmingly successful in financial terms, the *Lisieux* was laid up in Le Havre for the winter period, being put up for disposal in February 1966, and sold to Greek ship owner Agapitos Line and renamed the *Apollon*. She remained part of the Greek ferry scene until 1981 and was broken up the following year.

LORD WARDEN

The *Lord Warden* was the first stern-loading cross-Channel car ferry to be built for the British Transport Commission, and was specially designed for the Dover-Boulogne car ferry service. Following her withdrawal from service, the *Lord Warden* was sent to Newhaven for lay-up. She was hastily pressed into service to open the Weymouth-Cherbourg link in 1978, and she left the Sussex port for Weymouth in mid-March to open the seasonal route. The *Lord Warden* left the Dorset port on 20th March 1978 on the first Cherbourg crossing of the year, and she continued successfully on that route for three weeks,

making her final voyage from Cherbourg to Weymouth on 9th April 1978. The following year, she was put up for sale and purchased by Saudi Arabian interests. In 1979 Sealink sold the vessel for service in Saudi Arabia as the *Al Zaher*. Sadly two years later she was at the breaker's yard.

MAID OF ORLEANS

The *Maid of Orleans* paid her first visit to Weymouth on 19th July 1974 after one of the *Caesarea's* propellers became entangled in lobster pot wires in thick fog off St. Peter Port. The ship was immediately withdrawn for dry docking in Falmouth. The *Maid of Orleans* was hastily pressed into service, running 'light' from Folkestone to Jersey to pick up the timetable on the 20th July. The following day, she took the 13.30 departure from Weymouth, and returned direct to Newhaven from the Channel Islands. Her second spell in Weymouth occurred in July 1974, following the withdrawal of the *Sarnia* with turbine trouble. A Weymouth crew under the command of Captain Arthur Escudier collected the *Maid of Orleans* from Folkestone and she spent a

A classic view of the **Maid of Orleans** which made her first visit to Weymouth in July 1974. *(John Hendy)*

week on the Channel Isles' working, whilst the problems with *Sarnia* were rectified. In September 1975 she was laid up at Newhaven and later sold for scrap to a Santander breaker's yard.

MONA S QUEEN

One of the most interesting, and yet probably the most unsuitable, of all the ferries that worked out of Weymouth during the period under review, was the Isle of Man Steam Packet Company's *Mona's Queen*. She only appeared on the Weymouth stage in September 1989 because she was found to be totally

ineffective on the Sealink British Ferries Cherbourg service from Portsmouth. Although she had been chartered initially for that job, the *Mona's Queen* was switched from Portsmouth to Weymouth in exchange for the *Earl Godwin*.

In the late summer of 1989, the *Mona's Queen* made her first appearance in the English Channel, when she was chartered by the French Post Office for the start of Whitbread's Round the World Yacht Race. She anchored in the Solent with 700 sight seeing passengers on board, and then followed the competing yachts out into the English Channel. She was then